Access for All
Approaches to the Built Environment
Wolfgang Christ (Ed.)

With a Foreword by Thomas Sieverts

Birkhäuser
Basel · Boston · Berlin

This book has been kindly supported by Schindler the Elevator Company and Bauhaus-Universität Weimar.

Graphic design
Miriam Bussmann, Berlin

Translation into English
all texts except for contributions by Jonas Hughes, John Thompson /
Andreas von Zadow and Anna Rose / Tim Stonor:
Julian Reisenberger, Weimar

This book is also available in a German language edition
(ISBN 978-3-0346-0080-4)

Library of Congress Control Number: 2009930758

....

Bibliographic information published by the German National Library. The German National Library lists this publication in the Deutsche Nationalbibliografie; detailed bibliographic data are available on the Internet at http://dnb.d-nb.de.

© 2009 Birkhäuser Verlag AG
Basel · Boston · Berlin
P.O. Box 133, CH-4010 Basel, Switzerland
Part of Springer Science+Business Media

Printed on acid-free paper produced from chlorine-free pulp.
TCF ∞

Printed in Germany

ISBN: 978-3-0346-0081-1

9 8 7 6 5 4 3 2 1

www.birkhauser.ch

Table of Contents

Foreword
Thomas Sieverts

Access for All – a comprehensive design programme

It is a basic human right for people with physical or cognitive impairments to participate in social life. Nevertheless, access to the built environment is still not a matter of course. We are still far from achieving *Access for All* as an everyday quality of the design of our environment, although the path to achieving this aim has become clearer. The first advances were made almost half a century ago with a gradual shift away from the prevailing practice of segregating the physically and mentally handicapped from the rest of society. It began with the building of special care homes and special needs schools followed later by the installation of technical aids to overcome barriers in the home and urban environment and more recently the introduction of integrative measures in schools and at the workplace. Despite this progress, disabled people still face numerous difficulties. The basic human rights of people with handicaps are still far from being fully realised, and much still needs to be put into practice.

Over the last few decades, more widespread prosperity and tireless campaigning for policy reforms by the various disabled interest groups have raised awareness of accessibility aims and successfully pushed forward their implementation. The battle to improve means of physical access, such as ramps and lifts, to establish homes and schools for particular kinds of disabilities, and to end the discrimination of disabled people in the housing market has opened up a wider perspective of possible improvements and set its sights on a much broader notion of what constitutes quality of life: a new culture in which all people – regardless of their abilities or disabilities – should have equal opportunity not just to access the built environment but also to experience it fully.

The issue of "access" has since become a mainstream concern. General receptiveness towards the issue has increased, fuelled by an awareness that, as life expectancy increases, the probability that a normal-abled person may suffer from one or more disabilities in old age has increased drastically, particularly with regard to cognitive faculties as one's senses become impaired. We are all called upon to shape the architecture and urban design of our built environment from the house to the city as a network of diverse spaces with particular qualities that are generally accessible for everyone, without according certain individuals or groups any special status. If we are able to comprehend architecture as a medium for accessing and experiencing indoor and outdoor spaces with all the senses, we can look forward to a much more diverse built environment than we know today.

Ninety years after the founding of the Bauhaus, this challenges the dominance of classical modernism: the typical image of abstract, white, rectangular architectural compositions of light and shadows was an understandable and wideranging answer to the excesses of ornamentalism and the dark interiors of 19th century homes. At the same time, modernism's credo of rigorous functional separation and the radical optimisation of the individual functions stripped the environment of sensory richness.

By contrast, the principle of *Access for All* embraces an extended notion of access to our environment, one that engages all our senses. The integration of people with different abilities in a built environment that is open for everyone to use and experience, leads to the development of unusual design approaches that can be inviting and appealing for people of all age groups and abilities. As a result, everything that is devised and realised for these groups of people benefits the quality of the environment as a whole, creating stimulating spaces for "normal" citizens too. Children and young people, who have ever fewer opportunities for physical and sensory experiences as a result of the complete commercialisation of the city, will benefit particularly and directly from *Access for All*. However, this is not just about "access" in conventional terms; it encompasses a wider understanding of accessibility, for example with regard to accessing the Internet.

The collection of essays in this book offers insights into new directions in ongoing efforts to fully integrate people with different and/or restricted abilities. The challenge is to develop architecture and urban neighbourhoods that relate specifically to the physical characteristics of people and their senses, with the aim of establishing a kind of "resonance" between man and his environment. It is about finding an appropriate spatial and architectural expression for the ethical norms of equality.

Introduction
Wolfgang Christ

For more than half a century, access to the built environment has been associated with disability. Barriers have been identified and programmes of action put in place for their removal. What began as a minority group's campaign for greater assistance and recognition has developed into a civil rights movement. Specific building norms and design standards testify to the progress made and herald the gradual end of discrimination in the housing and employment markets, in the public realm, in modes of transport or in the handling of everyday objects. A laborious process is underway characterised by terms such as rehabilitation, equal opportunities and quality of life. In the built environment, the solution to the problem of access is the eradication of barriers – for the disabled.

This book takes a broader look at this issue. It proposes a new way of seeing and puts forward arguments for a paradigm shift in architecture where access is recognised as a structural challenge in the urbanised world of the 21st century. Today, access is a problem we all face and it has as many different facets and contradictions as the environment in which we live. The authors of this book examine this issue from a broad spectrum of different perspectives, reflecting on this experience from their respective professional backgrounds. For people who live with some form of handicap, access to the built environment is not just about the opportunity to take part, on their own terms, in the plethora of options available in the urban realm, rather this access is a matter of existential necessity.

The essays make it clear that a categorical demand for access "for all" will have significant implications, not least for the future role of architecture. It is foreseeable that architecture will have to fundamentally reappraise its very self-conception. In future, it will not be sufficient for architecture to be merely "free of" barriers to access. As a place, enclosure and medium in space, architecture will have to shed its passive role and actively support accessibility. Barrier-free building is a first stage, the training ground as it were, for a new conception of architecture as an *architecture of access* for everyone.

Access for All – Approaches to the Built Environment builds on international discourse on human rights, accessible building and products and services for the physically or mentally handicapped. Keywords such as *Universal Design, Design for All* or *Build for All*[1] characterise the current state of developments that first begun in the 1950s. The following represents a quick overview of key milestones of this process:

After the end of the Second World War, the USA was faced with the challenge of integrating thousands of invalid soldiers into employment

....

1 AG Angewandte Geographie/EDAD e.V. (ed.): *Von Barriere-freiheit zum Design für Alle – Erfahrungen aus Forschung und Praxis*, Münster 2007.

2 www.design.ncsu.edu/cud/about_ud/udhistory.htm
   Center for Universal Design, College of Design,
   North Carolina State University.

3 http://hsozkult.geschichte.hu-berlin.de/
   rezensionen/2007-4-025.

4 AG Angewandte Geographie/EDAD e.V.: loc. cit.

5 www.schindleraward.com.

6 AG Angewandte Geographie/EDAD e.V.: loc. cit.

and education. This marked the first systematic research into and subsequent development of assistive technology. In 1961 the first standards for barrier-free building were published, but it was not until 1991, 30 years later, that the "Standards for Accessible Design" were implemented as enforceable legislation. Civil rights for the disabled were first established in 1973 in the form of anti-discrimination laws, which came into force in 1977.[2]

In Germany, the 1970s were regarded as the decade of rehabilitation.[3] Building norms for the severely handicapped and wheelchair users were issued as well as planning guidelines for the disabled and elderly in the public realm.

In 1977, the European Council passed a resolution for the adaptation of housing and its immediate surroundings to the needs of the disabled. In 1981, the United Nations proclaimed the first ever International Year of Disabled Persons under the motto *Full participation and equality*. In 1981, the exhibition *Designs for Independent Living* opened at the Museum of Modern Art in New York, heralding an awareness of the legitimate market potential of people with restricted abilities. In 1993, the UNO proclaimed the 3rd December to be the annual International Day of Persons with Disabilities. In 1995, the Barcelona Declaration was agreed, after which the Catalonian capital city demon-strated by example its model qualities by initiating the "city for everybody" as an official programme, which it has begun to implement step by step.[4]

In 2003, the European Council proclaimed the European Year of Persons with Disabilities and with it provides the impetus for the *Access for All* student competition awarded by Schindler Holding Ltd., a Europe-wide competition that takes place every two years.[5]

This chronology of progress in the field shows that even in highly-developed, indus-trialised nations with democratic constitutions, it has still taken two generations to achieve societal recognition for what are essentially straightforward and self-evident qualities of life – for example, physical and legal accessibility – and to take appropriate action. However, we are still far from achieving Access for All! Rather, exceptions are more the rule. The fact that cities are able to actively advertise their accessibility credentials – for example Illingen in Saarland, Germany, or Esch-sur-Alzette in Luxembourg, the latter being the first town in Europe to have established an "accessibility plan" – makes the general dilemma painfully apparent.[6]

Access does not enjoy the status of a societal, economic, technical and cultural principle in the same way as sustainability currently does. Compared with Universal Design, *Green Building* is currently having a far more direct and wide-ranging effect on building and planning legislation, the building and property markets or energy and consumer goods industries. [7]

A possible explanation for the comparatively rapid implementation of sustainability for all – which started with the Agenda 21 summit in Rio de Janeiro in 1992 and now benefits from worldwide market promotion by organisations such as the US Green Building Council – could lie in the fact that the protagonists have been able to integrate "green" standards as an immanent part of the system, both in the economic and technical culture of modernism as well as in respective lifestyle milieus. Although sustainable development is a vitally necessary consequence of the unrestricted consumption of resources and the destruction of natural living conditions, it also seems that people are obviously convinced that the forces that brought about this problem will also be able to successfully resolve it.

Access for All can only learn from this: a successful implementation strategy will accordingly have to do all it can to implant the issue of accessibility as the next step forward in the canons of modernism – and with it leave a lasting impression!

In 2009, Weimar celebrated the 90th anniversary of the founding of the Bauhaus. The protagonists of modernism led by Walter Gropius were filled with a desire to find "absolute form". Instead of relying on convention, they relied on research. Their vision of a new architecture and a "city of machines and vehicles" as well as their "pursuit of ever more daring artistic means to overcome the effect and appearance of gravity", served as inspiration for people around the world who wanted to build a new and better world: for everyone!

The programme of the Bauhaus skilfully translated the fundamental principles of technical civilisation – division of labour, rationalisation, scientific methodology and media orientation – to the teaching and practice of architecture. Their declared intent to get to the root of things, to construct them so that they finally work "properly", to "free them from their respective individual limitations and to raise them to the level of objective design" remains, in principle, true to the present day. Nevertheless: the original promise of International Architecture to develop buildings "shaped by internal laws without lies and games"[8] was not able to append a clause to those "internal laws" grounded on instrumentalised reason and the primacy of progress, that anchors the right of all people to use and access their environment and the buildings within, independently and on their own terms, regardless of physical or mental ability.

Despite the ongoing hotly contested and controversial debate surrounding the Bauhaus

....

7 www.usgbc.org

8 Walter Gropius, *Internationale Architektur*, Mainz and Berlin 1981.

9 www.design.ncsu.edu/cud/about_ud/udhistory.htm Center for Universal Design, College of Design, North Carolina State University.

Style, the aesthetics of modernism can be conferred to architectural history. Not so, however, its structural principles with regard to construction and urban space, which to date have lost little of their power. It is here that industrial society, despite the fact that it brought forth a welfare state, proves to be ambivalent when it comes to the question of how much access it provides to the built environment. On the one hand, it aims to create – potentially for everyone – previously unimaginable rights and opportunities of access by helping the vast majority of the population to find adequate work and acquire modest wealth, and by providing humane housing, an abundance of goods, training and education, participation in culture and religion, mobility and health care as well as a reliable energy supply and clean water. As such, people's hopes to be liberated from restrictions have been fulfilled.

On the other hand, modernism was also responsible for erecting new barriers – a fact that can be attributed to its exceptional success – for example by appropriating the landscape as a space for living outside of the city. As the suburban way of life became more and more prevalent, so too grew the separation between living and working, living and shopping, and city centre and suburbia. Landscape was consumed. What started as suburbia for all has ended up in the USA as sprawl.

Mobility has taken on the character of work and necessity. Those who commute on a daily basis speak of lost time. Wealth and individualisation are slowly but surely loosening personal relationships with place, with one's neighbourhood, within the family as well as one's social class. The divide between young and old, rich and poor, and children and parents also takes on spatial dimensions that become ever more difficult to casually cross. Not everyone can come to terms with the speed of modernism. People who are less mobile become marginalised. In a figurative way this can equally be applied to modern means of communication and digital media. There is a clear divide between those whose command of new media allows them to integrate the potential of these technologies into their own work and everyday lives and those who only passively consume the internet. But the greatest success of the modern way of life, comparatively speaking, is the immense increase in life expectancy. At the beginning of the 20th century in the USA, average life expectancy was around 50 years; at the beginning of the 21st century, it is nearly 76 years. 85% of people today will live beyond 65 years of age. The number of 100-year-olds is expected to rise from 60,000 in 2007 to 214,000 in the year 2020.[9] As society as a whole grows increasingly older, handicaps will begin to be accepted as the norm and people will take note of the barriers that they themselves have erected, directly or indirectly.

In the foreword to the 2nd edition of *Internationale Architektur*, published in 1927, Walter Gropius spoke of the "purpose of new building as the design of life's processes." During the era of the Bauhaus, this could only be brought about by dismantling complexity, "[…] through the categorisation of all building elements according to the functions of the building, the street, the means of transport [and so on]."

Today, we must come to a conclusion that is diametrically opposed to the logic of functionalist modernism and its insistence on "objective design": in an age in which climatic change, demographic transformations, urbanisation and knowledge economies are the new paradigms and in which the global population is now three times what it was in the decade of the founding of the Bauhaus – currently almost 7 billion people, a number that looks set to rise to 9 billion by 2050 – sustainable development is dependent on compact spatial constellations with a complex mix of functions.

The success story of modernism is based on a rejection of the traditional city, which the German urban designer Klaus Humpert has characterised as the "container city."[10] In the industrial age it was not possible to master complexity in a compact form. Complexity at close quarters – a basic condition of the urban realm as we know it in Europe – must be designed contextually if coexistence is to be characterised by synergies rather than conflicts. Accordingly, as living conditions become more urban, architecture and access enter into an ever closer relationship.

In this book, the authors demonstrate access for all using current, prototypical examples. They show us which means of access to the built environment already exist today, which strategies have proven worthwhile and which measures are effective. We learn that access for all very often means more access for individuals with special needs and expectations – for example, when one wishes to reach one's destination in the megacity as directly as possible; when one wishes to help shape the quarter in which one lives or with which one identifies; when one wishes to have access to motorised transport that one can share with others; when one wishes to discover the happiness of being with the help of great thinkers; when one wishes to successively improve the comfort of everyday living in small steps or when one wishes to hear with the eyes and see with the ears in virtual space.

The series of issues and places in which emerging access scenarios can be examined is, of course, by no means exhaustive. Some important aspects are only touched upon or have not even been mentioned. A case in point is the im-

....

10 Klaus Humpert, Klaus Brenner, Sybille Becker, *Fundamental Principles of Urban Growth*, Wuppertal 2002.

11 Jeremy Rifkin, *The Age of Access: The New Culture of Hypercapitalism, Where all of Life is a Paid-For Experience*, New York 2000.

pending tendency to afford access only to those with sufficient privileges, that is to artificially restrict access in order to monetise the provision of access. Jeremy Rifkin was one of the first to point to this phenomenon in his book *The Age of Access*. One of his examples, described in the chapter *Access as a way of life*,[11] is the increasing privatisation of residential quarters in the form of Gated Communities, a phenomenon that is also becoming more widespread in Europe. These turn access into a consumer product for those who can afford to buy into the lifestyle on offer and are willing to relinquish their basic property rights. This has to be interpreted as a warning sign, as an attempt to escape from the complexities and contradictions of urban civilisation.

An *architecture of access* must, therefore, seek to enlighten and connect and must comprehend the built environment as an instrument with which one can achieve the aims of freedom, sustainability and beauty for everyone in the 21st century.

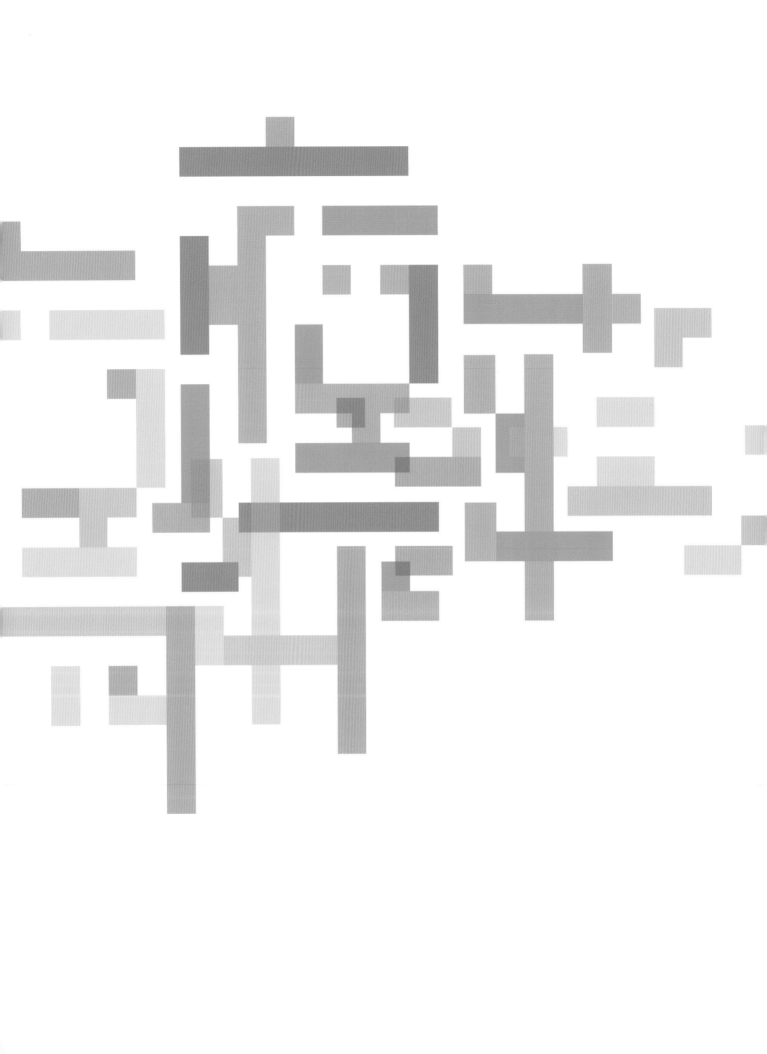

Elevation –
A cultural history of the elevator
Jeannot Simmen

The dream of conquering the vertical, of the ladder to heaven in Christian iconography, has become technological reality in the modern day. The elevator, our profane and terrestrial means of ascension, overcomes gravity and lightens our physical weight. However, the call for *Access for All* still remains problematic with regard to the vertical. Only with the help of mechanical aids are we able to overcome the perpendicular, whether with a ladder or a high speed elevator.[1]

Modern technological conveniences banish fatigue and exhaustion

"Amerika", a word evocative of promise and the dream of a new life, was the title[2] of Franz Kafka's unfinished novel in which he described the strangeness of a world far away. The protagonist, Karl Rossmann, is "dispatched to America" by his unfortunate parents "because a maid had seduced him and had a child by him".[3] On arriving in New York, the youthful hero espies the monumental Statue of Liberty from the ship and cannot help but mutter "So high". He stands in front of the high buildings in New York in wonderment, imagining how one needs an opera glass to look down on the street from the balconies above. Karl Rossmann soon finds a job in New York as a lift boy in a hotel. Within a week he is convinced that he has found his bidding in the service; he learns the art of a short deep bow

Max Ernst, "Baudelaire rentre tard", 1922, drawing in ink.

that is expected of lift boys and soon the tips come rolling in. However, a visit from a passing acquaintance, Delamarche, forces him to abandon his post causing him to transgress the "elevator regulations".[4] Fraught with bad luck and sought by the police, Rossmann seeks refuge in an acquaintance's upper floor apartment. "We are just above," said Delamarche once while climbing the stairs, but his prediction didn't want to come true, again and again the stairs set off in a new, imperceptibly different direction. Karl stood still, not so much out of drowsiness but out of helplessness against the length of these stairs. "The apartment is very high," said Delamarche as they went on again, "but that too has its advantages. You leave very seldom, you're in a bathrobe all day, we live very comfortably. Of course visitors never come this high."

The helplessness Frank Kafka describes when faced with stairs of such length accurately portrays an affliction of modern society, that of psychophysical exhaustion. Mechanical or visible injuries are not the cause but rather an invisible affliction of the nerves. Neurosis is a part of our body's defence mechanism for dealing with the new challenges of society.[5] Kafka's "Amerika" depicts the European apprehension of the vertiginous heights of the new world. New York's extreme heights represent a traumatic level of exertion for the gravity-accustomed body; without an elevator such heights hold the prospect of fatigue and exhaustion as a consequence of hectic life in the modern industrial city. Fatigue appears to be "a threshold value for the individual's adaptive capacity to modern society, a hindrance that needs to be eradicated."[6]

Until 1930, American skyscrapers were known in Europe as "tower houses" and described as solitary monuments in the manner of church spires. They were thought of as a mod-

Timber elevator cab, Lord & Taylor department store, New York, 1870; steam-powered lift by Otis with standing rope control.

ern-day successor to the cathedral: "The office tower is capable of the highest artistic effect, but it should only be permitted as a big exception that appears once only in a cityscape, as a town hall or single central commercial building," asserted Werner Hegemann.[7] In the metropolitan cities of the world, the elevator was hailed as a remedy: technology to counteract the hectic and mania of exhaustion. By 1880, the elevator had become a facility that "all comfortably furnished hotels in larger cities have begun to introduce."[8] The process of adoption was nevertheless slow and protracted: the elevator was initially quite controversial; its technology was regarded as being ugly, it did not fit inside buildings and was very expensive. It took decades for the elevator to be habitually adopted as a normal, modern and comfortable means of accessing first class buildings.

....

1   The modern elevator in the then tallest building in the world, the Taipei 101 Center in Taiwan (508m), can travel at a speed of 50km/h and reaches the top in 37 seconds. At such vertiginous heights "the strong winds … cause the tower to sway back and forth. One has the sensation of being slightly tipsy..." (Susanne Lenz, *Berliner Zeitung*, October 26, 2007). Since March 2008, the Burj Dubai, measuring 818m, is the

highest building in the world. It is due to be completed by December 2009.

2   Franz Kafka published the first chapter in 1913 under the title "Der Heizer. Ein Fragment" (The Stoker. A Fragment). In 1927 Max Brod edited the text and gave it the title *Amerika*. The alternative title "Der Verschollene" (in different editions translated as The Missing Person or The Man Who Disap-

Lift mechanism versus entrée and stairs, Paris, c. 1910; installation in the open well of a staircase.

Lift mechanism versus entrée and stairs, Paris, c. 1910; installation in the open well of a staircase.

While mechanical vertical transport made *Access for All* a reality for the tired and exhausted residents of the city, it also had an effect on architecture, in particular the ensemble of entrance lobby and staircase, once the calling card of a building. The introduction of elevators into upper middle class residential buildings reignited the conflict between the "École des Beaux-Arts" and the polytechnics, between the architects and the engineers. Ornate staircases found themselves competing with a piece of technical equipment which at the time was regarded as alien, mechanistic and ugly. The travelling platform, hoist and elevator represent the three technical stages of development for mechanical means of vertical elevation. Common to all three is that they transfer loads along a fixed channel. The load travels along a predetermined path or "hoistway" guided by rails or tracks. This fixed "channel" distinguishes elevators from other means of conveyance, such as a crane, travelling winch, cable car or ski lift.

Three inventions that contributed to the modern elevator

In terms of historical development, three inventions were responsible for the evolution of hoisting cages or goods lifts into the modern passenger elevator. These three inventions first made it possible to practically and comfortably reach the upper storeys of high-rise buildings. All these inventions were made in the second half of the 19th century; two are German inventions, one American.

....

peared) was mentioned by Kafka in a letter to Felice Bauer dated November 11, 1912.

3 Franz Kafka, *Der Verschollene*, edited by J. Schillemeit, Frankfurt a. M. 1983, pp. 7, 289.

4 The lift boy was "the lowest and most dispensable employee in the enormous hierarchy of the hotel's domestic staff", Kafka, op.cit., p. 213. Quote pp. 187, 225 ff.

5 Jeannot Simmen, *Vertigo. Schwindel der modernen Kunst*, Munich 1990, pp. 11 – 28; c.f.: Jeannot Simmen/Uwe Drepper: *Der Fahrstuhl. Die Geschichte der vertikalen Eroberung*, Munich 1984, pp. 57 ff., 136 ff., 220 f.

6 Anson Rabinbach, *The Human Motor: Energy, Fatigue, and the Origins of Modernity*, University of California Press, 1992.

7 Werner Hegemann, *Amerikanische Architektur und Stadtbaukunst*, Berlin 1925, p. 11.

8 Ibid.

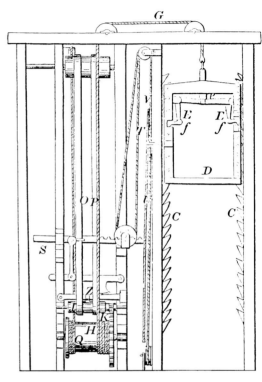

1. Vertical automatic safety mechanism – Elisha Graves Otis

Elisha Graves Otis was neither an engineer nor a wealthy industrialist but rather a typical American craftsman with a talent for tinkering. His invention was born out of an accident. After a mishap with a goods lift, E. G. Otis was asked to build a more safe device for vertical transport. What later proved to be his pioneering invention was the development of a special gravity braking system that prevented the fall of the hoisting platform in the event of an accident. Otis' idea, presented in 1853, comprised an automatic emergency brake, a self-activating mechanism triggered by gravity that was not dependent on human reaction. Patented in 1861, shortly before his death, his invention consisted of an automatic clamping mechanism that stops an elevator platform immediately and abruptly should its cable break, prevening the platform from descending at excessive speed.

Otis gave a public demonstration of his safety elevator as part of the World Fair in New York's Crystal Palace. Otis himself was both actor and stuntman and the presentation was suitably dramatic. At a height of about 15 metres above ground, he ordered the supporting rope to be severed by an assistant with a sword. No longer supported, the fully-laden platform fell momentarily before stopping automatically thanks to a

Automatic gravity braking system, Patent 31128, Elisha Graves Otis, 1861.

spring-loaded catch mechanism. Rem Koolhaas has described the spectacular demonstration as the epitome of "the non-event as triumph".[9] To be more precise, the triumph is the aversion of a more serious eventuality, as the snapping of the metal points into the timber runners prevented the occurrence of more fatal consequences.

This early automatic mechanism meant that elevator travel could be made safe, marking an iconic turning point in the history of the elevator. History records Otis' eureka-like pronouncement from the top of the platform high above the heads of the amazed audience: "All safe, gentlemen, all safe" – a phrase now syn-

Elisha Graves Otis demonstrating his free fall braking system in Crystal Palace, New York, 1854.

Elisha Graves Otis (1811–1861), the pioneer and founder of the lift empire.

....

9   Rem Koolhaas, *Delirious New York*, New York 1978, p. 19.
10 The elevator expert Jan M. Dulmno provides additional clarification: "With the exception of the automatic trigger mechanism, the arresting devices used later and in the present day differ entirely from Otis' invention in 1854. The triggering

criteria differs (excessive speed instead of cable failure) as does the braking mechanism (friction/wedge rather than snap-lock)…" (email to the author dated November 13, 2007). See also Andreas Bernard, *Die Geschichte des Fahrstuhls*, Frankfurt a. M. 2006, pp. 18 ff., in particular p. 26.

onymous with the safety elevator. History does not record, however, how Otis was rescued from the platform, as once wedged the platform could no longer be hoisted. In all probability, a simple ladder was used.

The automatic emergency brake was responsible for transforming the humble goods lift into a safe passenger elevator. In 1878, the braking system was perfected further by using a governor to trigger the mechanism once the speed exceeded 15–20% of the regular speed of descent. This was originally mounted directly on top of the elevator cab but is now located in a stationary position at the top of the elevator shaft and connected to the car by a second parallel cable inside the shaft. If the regular speed is exceeded, the governor causes this cable to be clamped, triggering the safety mechanism in the car. Nowadays, a softer braking mechanism is used to bring the car more gradually to a halt instead of the abrupt spring-loaded locking mechanism. The key word then as now, however, is "automatic".[10]

2. Heavenly ascension with the help of profane electrical power – Siemens & Halske

The second major invention that paved the way for the modern elevator is motorised power. Earlier steam or gas-driven motors were only suitable for use in factory sites where a steam en-

The first electrically-powered lift, a climbing elevator by Siemens & Halske, 1880.

gine could be installed, which in turn needed a machine operator to monitor the steam pressure energy levels. Water hydraulic systems

Panorama elevator, observers watch in amazement as the lift ascends without any apparent hoisting mechanism. Caricature from the year 1881 of the first electric elevator by Siemens & Halske.

were another means of powering elevators. They were most common in Paris where the inventor Léon Edoux had built large-scale hydraulic systems for the World Expositions in Paris in 1867 and 1889, which publicly demonstrated the use of those safe and smooth vertical elevators. Hydraulic systems were dependent on water under pressure which at the time also required steam-powered pumping machinery.

The advent of electrical power solved all these problems at once: it offered maintenance-free functionality and could be used more or less anywhere. Electric motors were also lighter and smaller than steam-powered motors. Electricity revolutionised the prevailing use of other sources of energy, although electricity itself is not a fuel in the same way as wood, coal, or oil is. Electricity represents a transmitted form of energy and became the medium of the modern age: power comes from the socket outlet! Electricity marks a paradigm shift: combustion processes without oxygen, heat without ashes. Electricity can be transmitted long distances, produced in the countryside and consumed in the cities.

In 1880, Werner von Siemens and the electrical engineer Johann Georg Halske demonstrated a new kind of vertical transporter at the Pfalzgau Exhibition in Mannheim, Germany. The platform of this new elevator device was neither pushed by piston nor hoisted by a cable. Instead it climbed mechanically, in a similar manner to a rack-and-pinion turned upright. The platform

was automatically mobile, the motor mounted beneath the viewing platform. What was disconcerting about this lift was that the runway ran straight through the platform and consisted of a ladder. The platform climbed up an outside wall and was an early form of the panorama elevator.

A contemporary caricature from 1881 shows the freestanding tower and climbing elevator. The caption notes ironically: "The viewing tower with dumb waiter for the heavens." Several details about the drawing are interesting: the spectators look high up in amazement, baffled by what is driving the elevator. They gaze with child-like wonderment at the artificial mountain towards the disappearing cab from which a passenger waves with a handkerchief. The wind whips a top hat from one of the citizens on high, the strong winds hinting at the lofty heights the machine is able to reach. The climbing elevator embodied a number of technical advancements and design improvements but its speed was still limited. The runway ladder was not without its dangers. Should a rung break, the cab would have fallen with considerable impact on the next rung and from there accelerated downwards. The electrical dynamo motor solved the problem of a suitable drive mechanism once and for all, however an efficient and safe transmission system was still lacking. But this had already been invented three years before the first electric elevator by another German engineer.

3. The mining industry finds a means to go very high by going very deep. Friction as a driving principle – Friedrich Koepe

The third revolution in vertical conveyor technology was discovered not by those wishing to ascend higher towards the heavens but by those wishing to descend ever deeper into the underworld. Vertical travel distances in the mining industry have always been greater than in building construction. However, as pit depths increased, the dimensions of the cable drum grew to reach a diameter of several metres. The successive unwinding of the cable from the drum caused the machine shaft and bearings to wear unevenly, increasing the risk of cable failure.

   To remedy this problem, in 1877 the mining engineer Friedrich Koepe (1835 – 1922) converted an existing drum-based machine for a 234-metre-deep mineshaft (the equivalent of an 80-storey building!) to a new form of drive mechanism. Instead of using a cable drum, Koepe fed the cable loosely around a large traction sheave. The cable was laid in a dovetail groove in its edge and propelled through traction. What appeared so simple and straightforward later also proved to be pioneering. However, it did not especially impress his employer, Friedrich Krupp, who failing to recognise its potential neglected to patent it. The mining engineer Koepe therefore applied for a patent in his

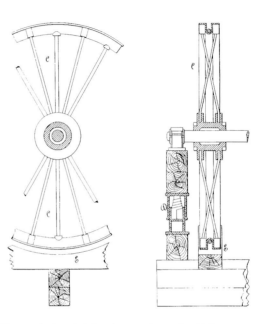

The rope is threaded directly over a large wheel (left) with a groove that holds the rope (right): traction sheave drive mechanism, patent specification 218, Friedrich Koepe, 1877.

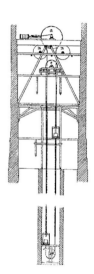

Traction drive elevator with additional sheaves to lessen the amount of rope wear and slippage. Design for mineshaft hoist, Hanover Colliery near Bochum, Germany, by Friedrich Koepe.

own name, which resulted in a dispute that caused the two parties to go separate ways.
The key principle was the use of "traction as drive". Besides the height of a possible fall, which at that time often exceeded 2000 metres, the miners descending in the mineshaft were fearful of three things in particular should the cable slide too quickly: the falling cabin often damaged the shaft casing, which then fell in behind them. Mine water collected at the base of the shaft; if the miners survived the fall they were

The Woolworth Building in New York, built from 1911–16 totalled 56 floors and was, until 1930, the highest building in the world. It employed state-of-the-art traction drive elevators.

likely to drown in the mud. The third danger was the cable itself, which fell down the shaft with such impact, that survivors might be killed by a fatal whip of the steel cable.

However, contrary to concerns, the new traction sheave mechanism was almost totally safe. As the length of the rope increased, so too did the friction reducing the risk of the cable slipping even at very long lengths. In the early 19th century, the idea of using traction as a means of driving a mechanism was regarded as pure lunacy. Accordingly the first locomotive, con-structed in 1811 by the British engineer John Blenkinsop used a cog rail, although it was on the level! The worry was that the iron wheels would slide on the rails.

Friedrich Koepe's brilliant and courageous invention solved several problems at once, and the individual elements of the construction are still used today: a parallel arrangement of trac-tion sheaves with multiple cables increased safety in the event that a cable should fail. As a result, the individual cables could be made thin-ner and more flexible. The cable was passed around the sheave only once reducing cable wear. By aligning the cable centrally, it was easi-er to calculate the tension forces at play and to eliminate the danger of cable slack. The latter was a common cause of accidents with the pre-vious cable drum drive: if a platform jammed on its way down, the cable would continue to un-wind, leaving the cage to fall unsupported once it dislodged. Finally, by ensuring an even distri-bution of tensile forces, the life of the cable, drum and motor could be prolonged. A so-called lower rope was used to evenly balance out the weight difference of the cables.

Without the modern elevator there would be no skyscrapers

The automatic safety brake, electrical power and safe transmission through traction were the

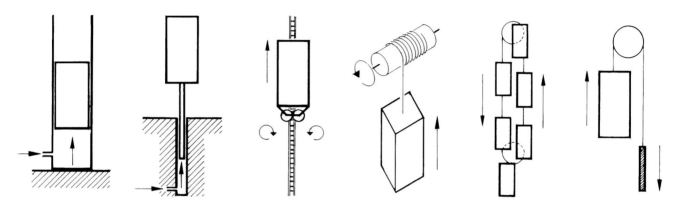

Schematic diagrams of lift drive mechanisms: air, water/oil, cogwheel/ladder, drum-hoist, paternoster, traction hoist.

three inventions that heralded the triumph of the modern elevator. They made it possible to travel to previously unimaginable heights within buildings. Travelling up and down with an elevator became safe and comfortable. In 1889, the word "skyscraper" appeared for the first time.

A major advantage of the combination of electrical power and traction sheave transmission is the limited space they occupy in terms of machinery and their light weight. The Woolworth building in New York, erected between 1913 and 1916, contained a series of elevators of this kind. Until 1930, it was the highest skyscraper in the world with the most modern and fastest elevator systems of its time. Its 29 elevators could reach a speed of 3.5m/s and a fast elevator could transport passengers 207 metres above ground. The continuing development of sky-

scrapers confirms the hypothesis that the height of buildings is largely dependent on advancements in elevator technology. The more efficient elevators were, the higher habitable buildings could be.

Elevator travel combines both modern and archaic experiences. It is modern because, unlike ship or rail travel, elevator travel does not entail journeying from place to place and offers nothing to see. Instead of passage over time, the relevant parameter is the time "wasted" while ascending. In an enclosed elevator car, encased in a concrete elevator shaft, the passenger is confronted with a series of uniform temporal experiences. The experience is also archaic because, whether alone or crammed in between other passengers, the elevator ride triggers an almost primeval sense of anxiety. The passage

Lifts and utopia: transparent lifts ascend in an architectural scene by László Moholy-Nagy in the film "Things to Come", produced by Alexander Korda, 1936, after the novel by H. G. Wells.

follows a prescribed vertical path, the car hangs on a single rope and the passenger is enclosed in a cramped space, usually without any view of the surroundings. The longer the journey takes, the greater the passenger's level of anxiety. An elevator ride becomes an experience that evokes archaic anxieties of helplessness and the loss of orientation and control.

Each person has an inner anthropological threshold. The equivalent to the absolute speed of light in modern physics is in everyday elevator travel the anthropological two-minute limit. A wait of around 30 seconds on working days and a journey time of about 100 seconds is generally regarded as tolerable. This tolerance level increases with the number of stops at different floors while passengers embark and disembark. This is generally also higher for residential buildings than office environments. Tourists are considered the most patient elevator passengers and, particularly when visiting attractions such as the Eiffel Tower or television towers, only rarely regard the journey as lost time or an enforced break. However, in the modern residential and office towers of 20th and 21st century megacities, elevator rides can take up to two minutes.

In addition to the duration of the elevator ride, the amount of space occupied by elevator facilities is a further limitation: the space required for elevator shafts increases disproportionately to the increase in available floor space

Marcel Duchamp, "Nude descending a staircase, no. 2", 1912.

with additional storeys. In buildings with conventional elevators, the proportion of space occupied by the elevator rises from 7% to 20% for towers with 70 to 100 storeys. There are three main possibilities for reducing the amount of floor space required for elevators:

- Twin car arrangements increase the capacity by around 30%. Again, this is a product of lessons learned in the mining industry. A tandem lift was installed in 1930 in the Sixty Wall Tower in New York (today the American International Building).
- The express/shuttle elevator is regarded as the most practical solution for buildings with more than 80 storeys. The building is divided into separate segments. Express elevators travel to transfer points – so-called sky lobbies – where passengers transfer to individual elevators for that particular segment. Sky lobbies often double as shopping or catering areas, sometimes also with fitness centres. The division into segments reduces the amount of space occupied by elevators in the building.
- Panorama elevators that ascend up the outside of buildings avoid the need for elevator shafts in the core of the building but also reduce the amount of window area. Nowadays, panorama elevators are often associated with prestige buildings. As sensational experiences, they also serve as a dramatic motif for films. In the past, they evoked a sense of utopia, as shown in the science-fiction movie "Things to Come" by Alexander Korda and H.G. Wells, whose futuristic model architecture was de-

signed by László Moholy-Nagy. The film is an optimistic counterpart to Fritz Lang's "Metropolis" (1927), in which slave-like workers were transported via lifts into the underworld to operate machines that kept everything running smoothly in the illustrious world above.

From 1980 onwards, the modern age goes electronic: it becomes international and global. Simultaneity, immateriality, and virtual environments begin to have a lasting impact on our habitual experience of reality. Our personal experience in local environments is haptic, in cyberspace telematic. This weightless, communicative form of "Access for All" takes place in a world we cannot experience as tactile reality.

The destruction of the twin towers of the World Trade Center brutally signified the sudden intrusion of reality in the year 2001: the hype associated with the dream of verticality was experienced as hubris in the very personal dimension of vertigo and fear of collapse. The elevator shafts in the World Trade Center became chimneys accelerating the fire; the kerosene ignited on all floors simultaneously, leading to the structural collapse of the so emblematic high-rise building.

The intrusion and collapse of reality: "It was like, raining people... You could watch them fall from like the 90th floor all the way down," re-

....

11 World Trade Task Force interview with EMT Michael Ober of October 16, 2001; New York City Fire Department, New York 2005.

called the paramedic Michael Ober, voicing his despair in the face of such verticality, "It's like you go to school for so long to be able to take care of people and treat them and be able to fix them when there's something wrong with them, and there's nothing, they hit the ground, and that's it. You just feel helpless, there's nothing you can do."[11] The vertical is turned into a fatal trap – indepently of how safe device the elevator is. The Mexican director Alejandro González In-árritu dramatises this in his film 11'09"01 (France, 2002), showing intermittent snippets between black film sequences with momentary glimpses of people springing, falling from the World Trade Center. New York, 11.09.2001: this date marks the end of the technical immunity of the vertical.

Today, the elevator is a technically sophisticated, safe means of transport. Electronic control systems optimise the utilisation of capacity, avoiding empty or individual journeys. The mechanical ensemble of power and transmission still uses the proven combination of electricity and traction sheave drive. Emergency braking systems still trigger automatically and use mechanical means. The elevator is the first mobile vehicle that doesn't require one to switch gears or depress an accelerator, that starts at the touch of a button, decelerates and stops with complete accuracy and opens and closes its doors on its own.

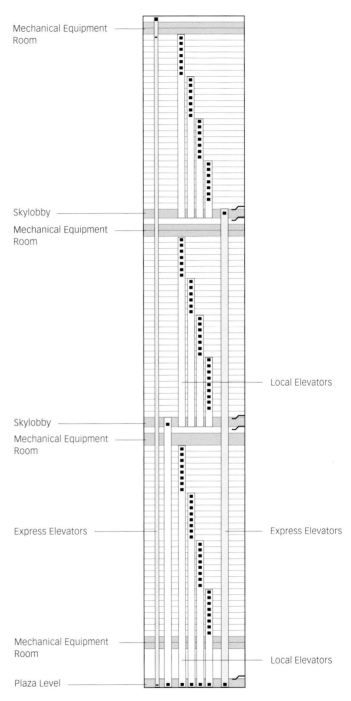

Schematic diagram of the lift arrangement in the World Trade Center, New York.

Megamobility –
Technology for the individual in the urbanised world
Jonas Hughes

New ideas are needed on how to apply existing knowledge.

The approach: those involved must look beyond their own objectives to a more encompassing view of the possibilities available.

With a few exceptions, travelling is one of the least pleasant experiences of being in a city. For motorists, the journey to work in the morning rush-hour is usually a bumper-to-bumper crawl along motorways that lead into ever more congested streets as one nears the city centre. Those who take trains must struggle into carriages that too become progressively more crowded, while bus passengers often have the added inconvenience of being stuck in inner-city traffic.

The experience of pedestrians is of crowded sidewalks and queues, polluted air, noise and the general discomfort of spending too much time on one's feet. And the pain doesn't neces-sarily stop there. Even in upmarket buildings with airy atria and glass façades, the journey from the ground to the upper floors can be in a crowded, windowless elevator which may stop an interminable number of times.

For the elderly, children or people with a disability, these problems may be magnified by obstacles such as stairs, busy roads with no safe crossings, or an absence of signposts or audio / Braille cues. The root cause is a lack of aware-ness of the access issues confronting substantial numbers of people. In Western Europe, around 15% of the adult population is estimat-ed to suf-fer from some form of disability, and these num-bers are growing as the society ages.[1]

The mobility problems confronting the world's cities are not in question. The time and energy wasted in traffic jams is variously estimated at tens to hundreds of billions of dollars a year for individual cities, while the environmental consequences of traffic pollution and the energy consumed for commuter journeys are widely acknowledged to be unsustainable. As the engines of global growth, cities are responsible for generating the lion's share of the world's wealth as well as the bulk of waste and emissions, a substantial proportion of which comes from automobiles.

Mobility problems in cities are often made worse by poor planning (or the lack of it) as well as too little investment in infrastructure. In many rapidly expanding cities of the developing world, mass migration to urban areas has overwhelmed city authorities, leading to urban sprawl, slums, pollution and gridlock. In the developed world, congested roads, over-crowding and no-go areas have come to be regarded as normal in the urban context.

City limits

One response of governments and local authorities to the gridlock has been to try and limit the flow of traffic into urban areas, for example, through congestion charges (in cities such as London), or by limiting the number of car licences issued (Shanghai). Such measures have had some success in easing inner-city congestion, but the impact is necessarily limited because they try to change behaviour without tackling structural deficiencies in urban design and transport. Also, a congestion charge for motorists entering a city centre, for example, shifts the burden on to the public transport network without necessarily a commensurate investment in the bus and/or metro system. The experience of London suggests congestion charges may also discourage people from travelling into the centre for leisure activities and shopping, harming local businesses.[2]

Another approach, tried in China, is to manage development of the urban environment by limiting the size of cities and their populations. This "structural" approach focuses on defining and enforcing city limits and designating new urban areas, or even whole new cities, so as to prevent cities' expansion from outpacing existing infrastructure and the authorities' ability to cope.

Such schemes look seductive on paper but tend to overlook or underestimate the actual

....

1   Eurostat: *Disability and social participation in Europe*, 2001.

2   London Chamber of Commerce and Industry, Response to the Consultation on the Proposed Cost Increase to the Congestion Charging Scheme, 2005.

3   McKinsey Global Institute, *Preparing for China's Urban Billion*, 2009.

The challenge: to make megacities accessible for individuals.

New mobility technology directs, integrates and connects.

dynamics of city development, as well as societal, political and financial obstacles. Shanghai's showpiece Pudong district, for instance, built on recovered farmland, rivals the skylines of New York and Hong Kong. But, at night, the streets are eerily deserted and the locals admire the lights from the other side of the river. A more ambitious project to build a completely new "ecological" city on nearby Chongming Island has so far failed to get off the ground after years of political wrangling.

In the meantime, China's cities – and especially Shanghai – are continuing to expand and the trend appears unstoppable. By 2025, it is estimated that six new megacities (with more than ten million inhabitants) will emerge alongside Beijing and Shanghai, and that these will be home to 13% of all China's city dwellers.[3]

The experience of China, and most of the developing world, is that cities evolve according to their own dynamics, and in spite of the best efforts of the authorities. Moreover, there is accumulating evidence to suggest bigger, denser cities are more viable and better at balancing the benefits and costs of urbanisation. The reason is because less sprawl leads to a reduction in energy use and pollution, and also because dense cities require less investment in public transport, infrastructure and services to make them work. A recent study of urban development in China over two decades showed bigger cities performing better on all measurements, including their impact on the countryside, and specifically waterways and farmland.[4] Indeed, the world's largest city, Tokyo, with over 35 million inhabitants, has been described one of the most intricately and carefully organised cities in the world, despite being nearly twice the size of the world's second-largest conurbation (Mexico City).[5]

With these insights, arguments that gridlock and mobility problems are best tackled by trying to limit the size of cities and using laws or tariffs to restrict movement cease to be persuasive. Instead, a more compelling argument points to a model of urban development that acknowledges the dynamic character of cities and instead focuses on making urban centres inclusive and attractive so that people choose to settle in them. The basis of this model is high-density environments, characterised by "multi-functional neighbourhoods," organised vertically, in contrast to lower-density clusters of single-purpose buildings, divided into "residential" and "commercial" areas.

Space as a continuum

The experience of the Schindler Group, a global mobility provider established in 1874, is that city planners, architects, and engineers have the necessary expertise and technologies to develop inclusive models of urban development. What is needed are new ideas about how to apply that knowledge, and for the protagonists involved to be able to look beyond their own objectives to a more encompassing view of the possibilities available.

Especially important is that all parties involved in design and construction consider their project – be it a building, a city block, a city quarter or a city itself – from the perspective of the people who will eventually inhabit the space. This means taking proper account of the needs of all inhabitants, including children, the elderly and people with special-access requirements. Equally, it is necessary to consider the activities of the inhabitants – work, leisure, shopping, entertainment, etc. – so that amenities and facilities are accessible and within a reasonable distance.

Historical attitudes mean that the planning and design process typically over-emphasises certain aspects of design and underestimates others. In the design of a building, for

....

4   Ibid.
5   Deyan Sudjic; quoted from Ricky Burdett, Deyan Sudjic (eds.), *The Endless City: Theory, Policy and Practice*, London 2008, based on the "Urban Age Project".

Modern urban mobility networks public and private spaces.

example, the emphasis is almost always on the use of space for commercial reasons (on the part of the developer) or for reasons of art, perception and mood (the architect). But space cannot meaningfully be considered independently of the means by which it is accessed. The occupant's perception of a space is always influenced by the journey into that space or vice-versa. If the journey was difficult, the space may be perceived as unwelcoming or alternatively as a place of sanctuary. The mood of a space will similarly influence the occupant's perception of the journey ahead. In extreme cases, the space may not be accessible at certain times or for certain people because of congestion or physical barriers.

Yet, on a typical urban development project, the mobility providers – in a building, the company providing the elevators – are usually selected only once the design is complete, since they are not considered critical in discussions about space. The building or development is in effect created independently of its mobility systems, which are seen as add-ons to be included once the structure is defined. This leads to paradoxical outcomes – buildings with elevators for wheelchair users which can only be accessed from the outside by stairs; plush hotels whose

Architects must concentrate on designing the city rather than individual buildings.

suites are located at the end of a long ride in a crowded elevator; crowded hospital lobbies where half of the elevators stand empty in case they are needed by staff or patients.

Many of these problems can be solved with traffic management and user-access technologies, which Schindler developed for both new buildings and existing ones. Other common design issues, such as "over-elevated" buildings – where capacity is planned for rush-hour conditions – can be avoided by the simple expedient of including the mobility provider in discussions during the early design phase.

In Schindler's experience, including engineers in the design process not only leads to an optimal configuration of elevators and escalators for a building, it also confers distinct benefits during the planning and construction phase. Typical examples are fewer shafts for the same or higher levels of traffic (in large buildings, elevator shafts can take up prodigious amounts of space); and more versatile design options for elevator lobbies. It may also be possible to use sections of the elevator shafts for the building's water/sewage and/or electricity systems.

A new design paradigm

The emerging urban landscapes of many cities consist of high-density developments combining multiple functions. Typically, shops, restaurants, and leisure spaces (parks, sport, and entertainment facilities) are located in a "podium" or open area at ground level, with residential apartments, offices, and hotel accommodation in one or more structures above. Underground there is usually a subway station, whose platforms are linked to the complex above by banks of escalators. Escalators are highly effective at moving large numbers of people from one level to another very quickly. And because their up and downward movement can be adjusted, they can be programmed according to the direction of the bulk of traffic – up in the morning, down in the evening.

Such structures, which may be large enough to accommodate tens of thousands of people, are a complete departure from the dominant urban model of single-purpose buildings located next to each other along a street. The horizontal configuration becomes vertical and in the process, the once almost inviolate distinction between residential, commercial, and retail spaces is lost. The transportation network – the equivalent of railways and roads – migrates indoors where the trains, trams, and cars are replaced by elevators and escalators.

The significance of this change is not to be underestimated. At a stroke, the public transport network for a "neighbourhood" of 20,000 people becomes the responsibility of the building management, which is directly accountable to residents and business tenants in a binding commercial relationship. This relationship extends to all "public" services within the structure.

The implications are equally significant for urban planning and design. Instead of designing a building, the architect must create a small city, complete with systems that combine mobility and access with varying levels of security, depending on the status of the person concerned – resident, office worker, hotel guest, delivery person, or visitor. The usual approach of designing a structure and "inserting" the essential systems at a later date is inconceivable. The new urban development will contain various mobility systems, from high-speed shuttle elevators with runs of hundreds of metres, to localised routes which serve smaller segments of the structure.

Intelligent mobility

Managing these mobility systems requires technologies capable of directing the movement of people and goods, controlling access to all spaces and connecting the mobility systems to those of the rest of the city. All elevators and escalators, as well as access routes, are managed by a central traffic management and user-access system, which plans journeys around the complex for all travellers, and takes account of each individual's mobility requirements, depending on their status (resident, visitor, office worker, etc.) and whether they have special-access needs.

Traffic management technology has brought a paradigm change to elevator travel. The first commercially available system was developed by Schindler in the 1990s, when the company realised that elevators would have to become more "intelligent," if they were to cope with the enormous flows of people, especially in urbanising Asia.

Schindler's traffic management system allows passengers to select their destination before entering an elevator, and then assigns them the car taking the fastest route (with the fewest number of stops) to their floor. The system is continuously updating its central database with the position of every elevator and every journey request, and uses sophisticated algorithms to calculate the optimum route for each passenger. As passengers select their destination floor, they are directed to "their" elevator using visual or (for the visually impaired) audio signals. Travellers with special needs,

Intelligent mobility systems "recognise" individuals and their destinations.

such as wheelchair users, press a special access button when selecting their destination to be assigned a larger car or an empty one, and for the doors to be held open for longer.

By linking all elevators in a building and optimising all journeys, the traffic management system allows the number of elevators (and therefore shafts) for a given building to be reduced while preserving the same elevating capacity. It also gives architects more freedom to place elevators in different areas or lobbies because passengers do not have to be able to see all the cars.

Secure access

As well as traffic management, mobility in multi-functional buildings requires systems that are able to control individual access and to monitor the movement of individuals within the building. Schindler makes this possible with Schindler ID, which combines traffic management with security, and access technology. The system "recognises" individuals and allows them fast and easy access to areas they are authorised to use.

With Schindler ID, everyone using a building is provided with a form of identification – for guests and visitors an access card; for residents and business tenants, a chip that may be installed in a card, mobile phone, watch or other item. The chip contains information about all the specific destinations and needs of each individual user. All entry points and elevators in the building are equipped with an interface. When the card or chip device is placed on the interface, the display shows all destinations which that individual is permitted to access. The users may then either select their desired destination by touching the screen. If they prefer the touchless option (perhaps for hygiene reasons), they simply wait as the display scrolls through the list of their possible destinations and then remove the chip device once the desired one is highlighted.

Because the user's information is held in a central database, the system is able to plan each individual's journey based on defined criteria. Hence, a resident of the building may select to always travel alone in an elevator when going to his apartment – in which case, the car they are assigned will not stop anywhere else, or for anyone else, during that particular journey. A visu-

ally impaired person will likely want always to be assigned an elevator that can be reached using tactile indicators.

By developing this technology, Schindler has made it possible for elevators to be quickly taken out of public use for a single private journey, and then immediately to be placed back into public service. Such a technology has numerous applications, not least in hospitals where – as mentioned – the elevators for visitors are typically crowded and in continual use, while those for medical personnel stand idle for much of the time. Another is in office buildings, where some elevators have historically been reserved for the use of top executives.

The future is here

The technologies and possibilities described above lie not so much in the future as in the present. The mobility and access systems referred to are to a greater or lesser extent already in place in thousands of buildings across the world. At the moment, they are operating in "isolation," which means they have yet to be connected to and incorporated within the wider urban environment, such as the public transport

From the world to the house: an integrated system of networked access technologies.

network. Their integration into the fabric of cities is a matter of time, not of possibility. In the future, access through the public transport network – from airport to apartment, for example – will be facilitated by a card or chip device that needs only to be swiped across an interface as the user moves from one mode of transport to another. Users departing for a particular location may be able to select their destination at the departure point, and thereafter be guided to the escalator or moving walk leading to the correct subway train or bus. Their connecting elevator and/or escalator and train or bus will be indicated on the interfaces they pass during their journey. On arrival at the destination station, the interface will pinpoint the escalator or elevator taking the most direct route to their floor. Residents returning home may choose to have their front door or office automatically unlock itself once the elevator delivers them to their floor. The door can equally be programmed to lock itself if they do not enter the space within a specified timeframe.

Cities evolve according to their own dynamics.

Cities have always defied planners' efforts to control them. As the birthplaces of civilisation and the world's engines of progress and economic growth, it would be surprising if they were easily tamed and controlled. A more realistic approach is to accept their dynamism and instead to focus on making their growth as habitable and pleasant as possible for the greatest number of their inhabitants, with intelligent, barrier-free mobility.

Cooperation –
Urban planning is a community project
John Thompson / Andreas von Zadow

A vision for the Liberties in Dublin

"Last night was very important for Dublin's oldest and most historic area – the famous Liberties," says Anne Graham, south central area manager, Dublin City Council. "On 2nd February 2009 at the City Council meeting, the councillors adopted the draft Liberties local area plan subject to amendments." This local area plan will now become council policy. Over the next decade it will guide the development of a 136 hectare area within south central Dublin. It is the direct result of a 14-month period of active engagement with the local community, which was kick-started by a community planning weekend in November 2007. Stakeholders came from all walks of life. There were long-term local residents, market traders, consultants, business leaders, and politicians. There were students and the elderly, there were experts and enthusiasts. The Liberties brought them together, along with a concern that this historic area of Dublin had somehow missed out on the boom years of the Celtic Tiger. Working together over the planning weekend, the community helped create "a vision for the Liberties."

From January to December 2008 monthly public community fora were held within the Liberties, accompanied by bi-monthly newsletters for every household, to communicate and inform people about the development of a high-

Dublin – the Liberties model demonstrates how new development will integrate with the existing urban fabric.

ly complex planning situation. During the autumn there was a formal consultation period in which the key elements of the planning framework were displayed, explored, explained and

Dublin – brownfield opportunity sites within the Liberties.

Area boundaries of the local area plan.

became the subject of submissions. Although there had been years of preparatory research about the physical and social conditions of the area, it was the active participation in a community planning process that has helped achieve an integrated urban development framework, turning the vision into a reality. This method of collaborative consultation has paved the way for billions of new investment from private and public sector projects in infrastructure, culture and commerce, media and technology, social benefits, residential developments, mobility, and environmental improvements. The Guinness brewery, which has been closely connected with the Liberties for over 250 years, is a key Dublin industry located at the edge of the local area plan. It will use the impetus of the

Liberties regeneration to rationalise landholdings and upgrade its brewing facilities.

The decision was made to provide access for all to the planning process at a very early stage. The draft plans were then amended, altered, and improved by ongoing public debate. Proposals were tested, changed, and tested again to get the best possible result in terms of urbanism, and at the same time the best possible consensus between local residents, project developers, property owners, elected politicians, planners, and other specialists. Participants included numerous representatives of Dublin City Council, who had the courage to commission this unique process of planning with ongoing public involvement. The success of the Liberties project provides an exemplar for Ireland. The

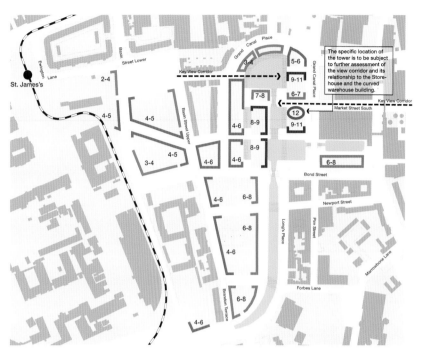

Dublin Liberties – diagram illustrating permitted heights for new buildings on brownfield site.

Number of storeys (estimated storey heights: ground floor, 4 metres; upper floors, 3 metres).

15 +
11 – 15
8 – 11
6 – 8
4 – 6
3 – 4
2 – 3

participation process was transparent and fully accessible to everyone. It has saved years of antagonistic debate. The result is a realistic and integrative planning framework, which can deliver regeneration, new developments, and ultimately good urbanism with spaces, places and, most importantly, life.

Participation rather than consultation

The Liberties project shows how collaboration with the community can be used effectively to inform and advance a statutory planning process. I would like to explain the principles and practice of a community planning approach to development and design. Terminology is all-important. In particular a distinction has to be made between "participation" and "consultation." In general, the word "involvement" is used to cover all forms of community engagement, but in more specific areas "participation" is used in relation to vision-building processes, and "consultation" to describe involvement with formal proposals. Often these terms are used interchangeably, when in fact they describe two very different modes of community involvement. Participation involves people taking part and sharing in a process that sets the agenda for the future development of an area. It requires an open forum in which all local stakeholder views are given equal consideration. A good participa-

tory process will engender consensus-building, help reconcile differences, and create a dynamic, inclusive vision for the future that garners a shared sense of ownership. Participatory events are important not only for their outputs, but also because they help to enhance social capital by bringing communities together in a positive way, revealing shared values, mutual interests and common goals. Consultation differs from participation because it is about an exchange of views. It has a more restricted scope than participation and involves a community being brought to an understanding of formal proposals and then given the opportunity to present their views on how well these measure up against the aims and objectives that have already been agreed and set in place for development within their local area.

It is a lack of understanding of this distinction that has led many private developers (and some local authorities) to resist community involvement because it is perceived as a highly confrontational forum without positive benefits. But this hostile response almost invariably stems from the same root cause – that local communities, even though invited, have not participated in the production of their local plans. When local people are consulted on formal proposals, they become frustrated that discussions about alternatives are not on offer. Hostility arises because they are presented with the restricted scope of consultation, when what they really want is an open process of participation.

This persistent practice of presenting communities with what amounts to a fait accompli has seriously undermined people's trust in the present planning system. In our own work, we repeatedly encounter communities incredulous of the fact that the formal proposals they oppose are actually in accordance with planning policies guiding development in their own neighbourhoods. As a result, planning committee members find themselves caught between the policy-based advice of the local planners and the highly emotive feelings of the communities they have been elected to represent. At this point, schemes are repeatedly deferred or rejected without material grounds, only to be lost at appeal. Whilst this may be good for the legal profession, it is clearly untenable for a government looking to private finance to deliver the development the country needs in order to remain prosperous and offer a better quality of life. At present there is no best practice guidance for community involvement, and, more worryingly, a distinct lack of experience, skills, and resources within most local authorities in the United Kingdom.

Community involvement: how it can be done and why it works

Community involvement is a complex field of study because there are a myriad of different approaches being undertaken by practitioners from a wide variety of disciplines including planning, urban design, architecture, and landscape design. In his publication *The Community Planning Handbook*, Nick Wates lists over 50 of these strategies such as community planning, action planning, hands-on planning, urban design studios, and community charrettes. The scale of engagement within these can also be extremely varied and range from large-scale regional planning issues down to very small scale and specific proposals for neighbourhood facilities such as children's playgrounds or pocket parks.

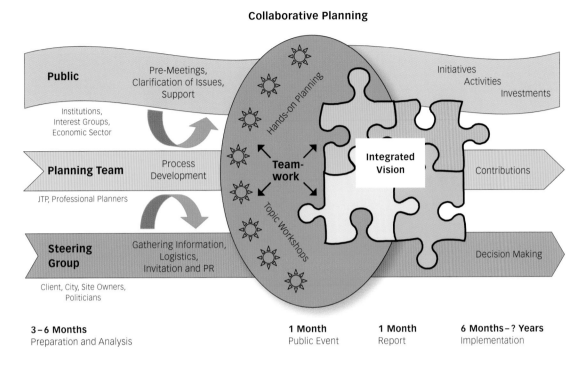

Collaborative Planning

The collaborative planning process – the planning team facilitates a creative process that involves decision makers, other stakeholders and the wider public in developing an integrated vision.

It's all about "contribution"

What they all have in common, however, is that they provide local stakeholders, including the residents, business people, service providers, local authorities, and a variety of interest groups, with an opportunity to contribute to the development process. As advocates of the process, we believe that everyone who lives or works in a particular area has something to contribute towards shaping its future, and we have learnt that by involving them from the outset it is far more likely that local neighbourhoods will receive the type of development and services that they really need to prosper. We have been in-

volved in what we term "community planning" for more than a decade and have carried out well in excess of 100 exercises throughout the United Kingdom and across Europe. Initially our commissions tended to come either from the public sector (local authorities/regional development agencies) or from community groups backed by government money. Often these projects were located in problematic areas suffering from severe deprivation that required serious physical, social, and economic regeneration such as parts of Manchester, Newcastle, and Belfast. In the last few years, however, private developers have begun to see the financial and other benefits that can accrue from community planning. Although our approach to community involvement is constantly evolving, in recent years we have developed a four-stage approach that has been widely acknowledged as delivering impressive results.

1. Project start-up and community animation

The lead-in period for a community planning exercise can range from a few weeks to several months, depending on the scale and nature of the project. Working alongside a commissioning body, we generally start by establishing a steering group that includes local council members, important members of the local community and business people who help to develop the scope of the project. One of the essential aims during the first stage is to ensure that the widest possible spectrum of people attend the public event itself, which may only last two days. The importance of animating the local community, of making them aware of the event and the significance of their personal contribution, cannot be underestimated. Our approach to this has become more sophisticated in recent years and goes well beyond the traditional use of mail shots and posters, and now involves our team literally "putting the word on the street" by encountering the local community in-situ, at residents associations, local interest groups, arts and cultural associations, civic and local history

Chichester Graylingwell – visualisation of a key public space.

societies, youth clubs, business forums, and schools. Once the message has begun to circulate on the ground, a Launch Event will be used to focus media coverage, reinforce what is being asked of local people, and emphasise the implications it will have for their quality of life in the future. In a world of intense competition for people's attention, animation has to have both the visibility of a marketing campaign, as well as the credibility that derives from word of mouth communication.

2. Vision building

The second stage has by far the highest profile for local communities and involves a large-scale participatory event. During this, people of dif-

Chichester Graylingwell – new sustainable neighbourhood on a disused hospital site.

Vision drawing of the carbon-neutral settlement.

Conversion of existing heritage buildings to new uses can underpin regeneration.

ferent ages, backgrounds and cultures, with different concerns and enthusiasms, get a chance to listen to each other, to offer suggestions and to enter into a constructive dialogue. These discussions are facilitated by a neutral, multi-disciplinary team, with a range of skills and experience that are specific to the nature and particular characteristics of the project. This will include our own community planners, architects, and urban designers, as well as a range of specialist collaborators that might include business analysts, funding experts, civil and traffic engineers, hydrologists, landscape designers, and ecologists. They arrive with open minds and a blank piece of paper, prepared to listen and learn before using their own professional skills to help transform the aspirations of local people into a viable vision. On the day before the public workshops the professional team familiarises itself with the site and location and receives background briefings from key people drawn from the local authority, resident groups, business associations, and interest groups. The public workshops generally take place over two days including a Friday, to enable local schools to participate, and Saturday for people that are working.

The aim of the public sessions is to tap common intelligence and create value for everybody. Despite apparent differences at the outset, conventional boundaries soon break down, releasing imagination, positive thinking, and collective creativity, out of which a consensus almost always emerges. The participatory

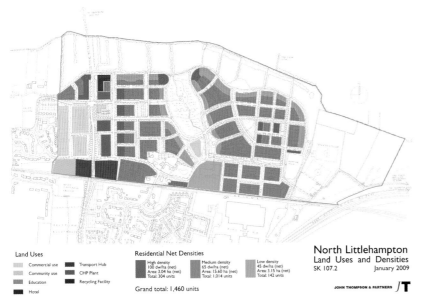

Land Uses

Commercial use
Community use
Education
Hotel

Transport Hub
CHP Plant
Recycling Facility

Residential Net Densities

High density
100 dw/ha (net)
Area: 3.04 ha (net)
Total: 304 units

Medium density
65 dw/ha (net)
Area: 15.60 ha (net)
Total: 1,014 units

Low density
45 dw/ha (net)
Area: 3.15 ha (net)
Total: 142 units

Grand total: 1,460 units

North Littlehampton
Land Uses and Densities
SK 107.2   January 2009

JOHN THOMPSON & PARTNERS JT

Sustainable urban extension at North Littlehampton – land use and density.

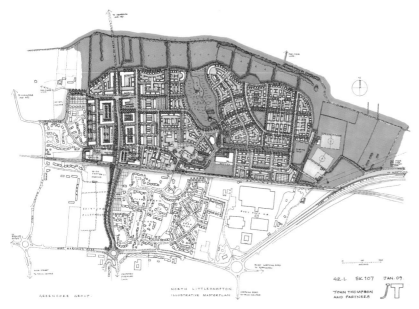

North Littlehampton masterplan for a new mixed-use area on an ecologically sensitive town site.

processes we employ most frequently are "future workshops" and "hands-on planning." The former of these addresses specific local issues that have been identified in advance. These might include housing, education, health, business, young people, green issues, recreation, and transport. Occasionally a number of local people might feel an additional issue should be addressed and impromptu workshops can quickly be organised. In the workshops the facilitators are trained to carry out a three-stage process. It begins with a "problems session" that allows for a critical stock-taking of the present situation during which negativity is drawn out and local people are allowed to "get things off their chest." This is followed by a session entitled "dreams" in which people are then asked to use their imagination and say how they would like things to be, whether they be environmental improvements, new facilities, services or forms of employment. Finally, those taking part are asked to consider solutions – how they might go about achieving their aspirations and who might fund them. This concluding part of the workshop is often a learning moment for the participants – they know what they would like – but few understand the mechanisms for delivery. At this point the professional team will use their expertise and stimulate the debate by suggesting funding streams and management possibilities as well

North Littlehampton – hand-drawn vignettes illustrating the character of key spaces.

as providing supportive anecdotal evidence of how dreams have been achieved elsewhere.

During these sessions participants contribute by jotting down ideas on post-it notes, which are then read back to them before being grouped into themes or categories. The lead facilitator may request further information or clarification and engender discussion, but the most important aspect of this is being seen to listen, to seek local knowledge, and to treat all viewpoints equally and with respect. The use of post-it notes is a subtle strategy of inclusion, which grants everyone the same voice and diffuses the potential for aggressive argumentation on single issues of dissent. In this way the loudest voices often become overwhelmed in a sea of quiet consensus. Unable to dominate the proceedings when asked to write it down, militant

individuals often leave and open the way for constructive discussions.

Over the years, our approach to facilitation has gradually evolved as we have learnt to take account of more aspects of human nature. Facilitators moving amongst the participants are always on hand to put people at their ease, explain what is happening or offer advice. They act like a lubricant, easing viewpoints out of people who are initially uncomfortable with the situation or unsure of what they are being asked. They are also alert to the fact that statements such as "I've forgotten my glasses" can be euphemisms for illiteracy – and a trigger for other approaches to allow these people to make a meaningful contribution. At the end of a morning or afternoon session all the topic groups that have taken place meet together for a plenary

Collaborative planning process

Contributors to the process.

session. One or two participants in each group will work with the facilitators to create a flip-chart summary of the points of consensus including a list of the most important issues, and a series of "action points" that combine aspirations with methods of delivery. The report back sessions ensure that everyone attending the event is aware of the range of ideas and options that are emerging, and further comments and ideas from the floor are added to those already generated. The presentations are invariably by topic group participants to reinforce the fact that these are local people's ideas, and engender a greater sense of collective ownership.

The second type of workshop that produces valuable material is "hands-on planning." The

themes for these sessions often emerge out of the topic groups, and are then developed into a more physical form, working in small groups around large-scale plans of the area. Architects, urban designers, and other professionals are present to assist and facilitate these sessions, but participants are encouraged to work out potential solutions along with others who may or may not be in agreement. Responsibility is passed to the participants to try and reach consensus amongst themselves. The result of these "hands-on planning" sessions is a number of visually stimulating plans which have been designed on a collaborative basis, combining community aspirations with commercial realities. Where appropriate these exercises sometimes

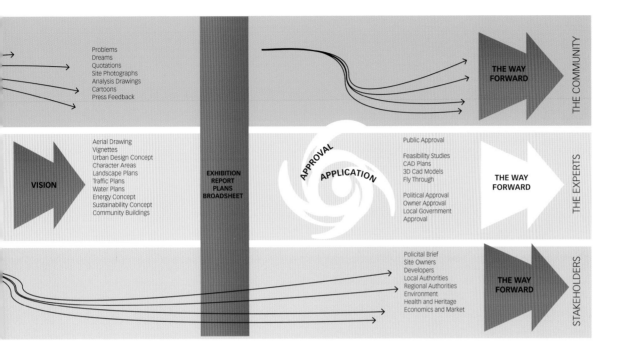

develop into walkabouts, when professional team members will accompany participants to areas of particular concern. These are particularly powerful techniques of community involvement in which local people literally lead the way, and data is collected in a variety of forms by mapping, photography, or records of conversations. Walkabouts are highly visual affairs and frequently gather up participants as they progress and engage with people where they feel most comfortable – in their own neighbourhoods. Once again plenary sessions help to communicate the range of ideas coming forward and the professional team assist in highlighting areas of consensus, facilitating discussions around issues or proposals that require

further consideration and mediated solutions. Towards the end of the two public days a "way forward workshop" is held to discuss how the development process can be taken forward. For community involvement to be successful it is vital to maintain momentum and ensure that there is an ongoing role for the energy and sense of common ownership built up over the course of the participatory event. At the close of the public sessions the huge task of assimilating all the information begins. In addition to the material from the workshops, other team members will have been carrying out urban design, economic and landscape assessments of the area under scrutiny. The way a place can change over time and its historic significance will also have

Caterham Barracks, Surrey, a disused military site.

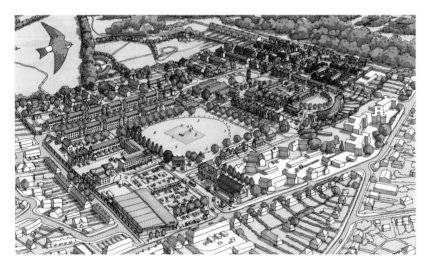

Caterham masterplan after the cooperative planning process: higher density, new jobs, many more new homes with a successful community development trust – a great success story for private sector development.

been researched. Over the following days the professional team works in private, analysing and evaluating the output from the public sessions, and building a deliverable vision for the area that meets with the aspirations of the local community. This vision is reported back to the participants within a week of the start of the event.

Speed is of the essence as most communities have grown weary of endless, drawn out bureaucratic processes that rarely reach meaningful conclusions. This presentation prepares local stakeholders for the vision by recounting the process they have just participated in, with images of topic groups, hands-on planning, plenary sessions, and walkabouts together with summaries of all the workshops. These are intercut with verbatim quotes from local people that illustrate the major points of consensus. Finally, the vision is unveiled with a conceptual masterplan illustrated with sketches and vignettes that give an impression of how things could be in the future if the public, private, and community sectors work towards a common goal. A delivery mechanism is illustrated using approachable metaphors and cartoons rather than abstract diagrams. An associated exhibition provides the focus for further discussion later in the evening, a broadsheet publication provides a brief synopsis of the vision for people to take away, and briefing packs are made immediately available for the media.

3. Focus groups and project development

In the early years of community planning, many projects faltered after the vision stage. This was often due to a lack of continuity or commitment at a higher political level that meant funding streams could not be put in place to carry out the proposals or even take them forward to the point where local plans could be altered to better reflect community aspirations. In recent years this has begun to change as private developers have begun to recognise the benefits that can accrue from involving the local community, particularly on contentious sites. Once private finance began to drive participatory processes, remarkable results were achieved and an entirely new set of techniques had to be devised to carry projects forward. For this third stage of community involvement we tend to favour the use of focus groups, as has been demonstrated with the Dublin Liberties project. These are generally set up at a community forum held soon after the presentation of the vision and vary in nature according to the type of project and the interests of the participants. Typically these might address Agenda 21 issues, recreation and sport issues, cultural issues, approaches to her-

New homes for sale and rent at Caterham.

itage, health and education, employment concerns, local business, or tourism opportunities. These groups meet at frequent intervals with the design team to advance thinking in specific areas and to share their ideas and viewpoints. These are fed back into the master planning process and frequently affect the development of the project. This iterative process ensures that by the time formal proposals are submitted for planning consent, local stakeholders feel a strong collective sense of ownership, and objections are far less frequent.

At Caterham Barracks in Surrey we ran a large-scale participatory process involving over

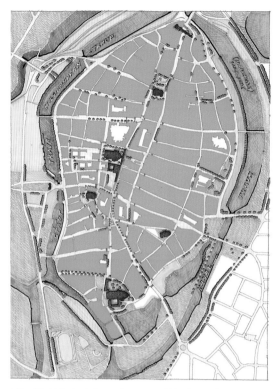

Lübeck's historical city centre – a world heritage site.

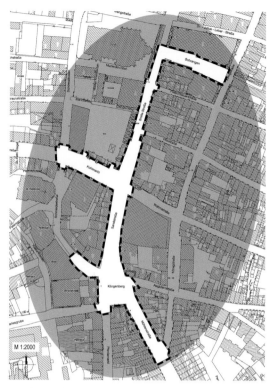

Boundary defining the central public realm that is to be redesigned.

1000 participants including local residents, businesses, schools, the planning authority, and various interest groups. The consensus vision that emerged overturned the local authority's brief for the site, which had essentially rendered the development of the former Ministry of Defence site economically unviable for private finance. During the community planning event local people accepted that, in order to deliver the level of benefits they required, additional enabling development would be necessary. This opened the way for an additional 300 residen-

tial units to be built on the site. Following the event a number of specialist focus groups were set up to continue the dialogue, and involved over 100 local people meeting up on more than 50 occasions.

4. Transferring ownership

The final stage in a participatory process is possibly the most important in terms of the long-term sustainability of a project, and involves the establishment of one or more legal entities that

Lübeck – proposal for new café at Schrangen Square, winning competition entry by the office Petersen Pörksen & Partners.

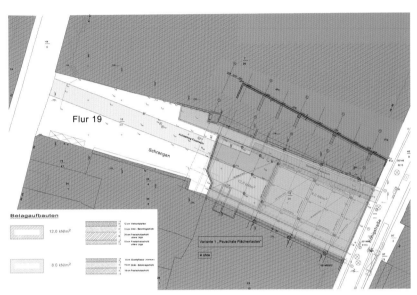

Technical conditions limit possibilities for new buildings in the square.

assume control of the community assets. These can vary and might include Community Development Trusts that own and manage community facilities, Social Enterprise Trusts that look after business initiatives or Environmental Trusts that might be responsible for parks or recreational facilities. At Caterham Barracks over £5 million of assets have been transferred into the ownership and management of these vehicles, set up with a financial contribution from the developer. They include a nursery, bar/restaurant, dance studio, health and fitness centre, meeting rooms and Skaterham, a highly successful indoor skateboard and BMX centre for young people which hosts international competitions and has over 6,000 members.

Overview

When our team arrives in an area, they have no history of involvement, no hidden agenda, and no personal attachment. We are able to empathise and criticise in equal measures, and usually gain the trust of the event participants

Lübeck – view into the main pedestrian route Breite Straße before the renovation.

Proposal for redesign of the central, highly sensitive space as result of a cooperative planning process "Mitten in Lübeck".

within a matter of hours. This is only possible because of our perceived neutrality – a status that in our experience is rarely conferred on local authorities by the communities they represent. Community involvement can turn criticism into a constructive dialogue. It allows local people to understand each other's concerns within a broader context, and thereby make decisions that are based on collective aspirations rather than narrow personal desires. Community involvement can quickly establish a consensus vision for an area. It can also help identify appropriate mechanisms for the delivery of this vision including potential development partners and funding streams. It creates joined-

up thinking and joined-up action. Currently development practices often proceed in a piecemeal fashion, in accordance with local plans that are frequently outdated within months of being published. Such schemes serve their own ends and often close down other more exciting or beneficial possibilities.

Contrary to popular belief, engaging in community involvement is not like opening Pandora's box. By creating a consensus view amongst stakeholders, development can proceed through the planning system unhindered by opposition, and achieve results that traditional methods may take many months or even years to produce. Community involvement provides a fast track learning process for all the participants. This helps ordinary people understand the development process, the issues that face their local community and the barriers that stand in the way of fulfilling their aspirations, such as economic viability and funding logistics. Community involvement unlocks the energy and enthusiasm of people in the local community. It can inspire individuals to take on new responsibilities. In this respect it supports capacity building, local democracy and encourages good citizenship. It also provides projects with strong advocates who help carry the vision forward because they feel collective ownership of the proposals that will have a beneficial effect on their quality of life.

....

Further reading

Nick Wates, *The Community Planning Event Manual*, Earthscan Publications Ltd, London 2008.

Nick Wates, *The Community Planning Handbook*, Earthscan Publications Ltd, London 2000.

Andreas von Zadow, *Perspektivenwerkstatt*, Deutsches Institut für Urbanistik, Berlin 1997.

Andreas von Zadow, "Konzertierte Aktionen für einen integrativen Stadtumbau," in: *Stadt im Umbau – Neue urbane Horizonte*, Salzburger Institut für Raumordnung und Wohnen, Salzburg 2005.

Selected websites

Liberties Regeneration – Development of a regeneration concept for an urban quarter on the Guinness brewery site, 2008–2009
www.theliberties.ie

Village at Caterham
www.communityplanning.net/casestudies/casestudy009.php

Community planning workshop "Mitten in Lübeck" (In the centre of Lübeck)
www.communityplanning.net/casestudies/casestudy008.php

Graylingwell, Chichester – Conversion of a former listed hospital complex to a carbon-neutral mixed-use settlement, 2008
www.graylingwellchichester.com

Northlittlehampton – New neighbourhood on the north edge of Littlehampton 2008
www.northlittlehampton.org

Community Development Trusts
www.dta.org.uk

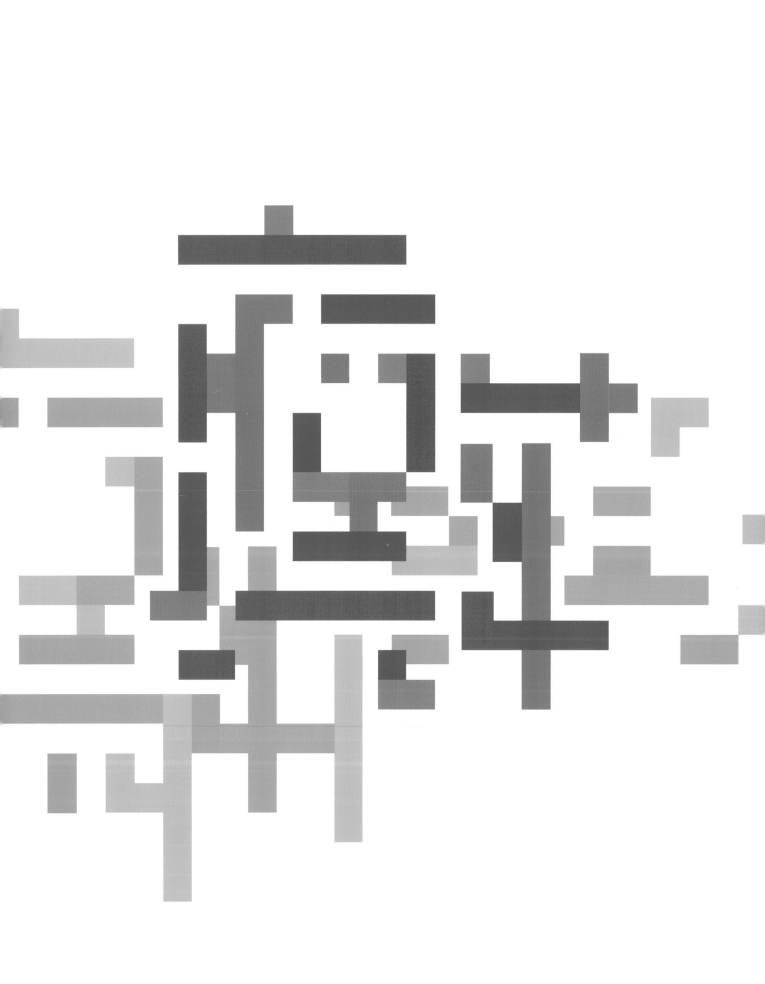

Variety –
The Südstadt in Tübingen as a model for the city
Cord Soehlke

In the 21st century, more people now live in cities than in rural areas. In western societies in particular, people's everyday lives, and what they can and cannot do, are shaped by their urban environment. This apparent triumph of the city cannot, however, be attributed to a single model of the city but rather to a bewildering assortment of urban concepts and developmental processes. The much-vaunted European city – with its compact, diverse mix of functions – is now no longer the dominant form, both in terms of quantity and influence, and has been relegated to a less relevant branch of urban practice. Since the 1950s at the latest, the ideal of the functionally separated, zoned city has dominated. Theoretical discourse too was similarly convinced that the future lies in the "city without qualities" (Rem Koolhaas), the post-city, the vertical city and the suburban city – urban typologies that flourish without the dense mix of functions and qualities that characterise the European city.

Despite such gloomy prognoses, in Germany and Europe a gradual renaissance of the urban realm has started to emerge since the late 1990s. Ever more cities have created and are creating opportunities for residents and businesses to move back into the inner cities. What do people expect from life in the city? What motivates families and businesses to point their removal van towards the cities and choose an urban en-

Old and new in the Loretto Quarter.

vironment? A comparison of two different development models aims to offer some answers: on the one hand, the development of the Südstadt district in Tübingen, a pioneering urban renaissance project, and on the other, a (necessarily generalised) look at the suburban developments in southern USA. A fundamental prin-

Residential neighbourhood in Riverside, California.

ciple of this comparison is the ability, or the privilege, of the city to offer *Access for All* – access to everyday culture, interaction and participation in social life for as many people as possible.

Building cities rather than settlements

Since the mid 1990s the university town of Tübingen has been redeveloping a site previously occupied by military barracks to create a new neighbourhood for 6,000 residents as well as 2,000 workplaces. Alongside local aims, such as upgrading the comparatively deprived Südstadt district and alleviating pressure on the local housing market, one aim was clear from the outset: to build a piece of city, not a housing set-

tlement. Four key concepts form the basis for the (then almost audacious) attempt to convert an abandoned site into a functional urban environment:

Mixed-use, dense, urban – and nevertheless attractive?

The basic typological element of the development is an urban townhouse with apartments on the upper floors and shops and commercial premises on the ground floor. In 2008, the Loretto and French Quarters, the first two quarters to be completed, contain more than 200 shops, offices, workshops and facilities providing almost 1,000 jobs. The intention of this mixed-use concept was not only to stimulate an open and lively atmosphere of the kind that can only come about through functional diversity but also to create many high-quality jobs. An equally important aspect that becomes increasingly important over time is that diverse functional provisions make it easier to organise one's everyday activities. The close proximity of workplace, childcare facilities, shopping, culture and restaurants, sometimes even within babyphone reach, facilitate a more flexible and attractive living arrangement. A further important element of mixed-use concepts is the programmatic integration of social and cultural infrastructure in urban quarters: children's nurseries, adult education centres, disabled projects and social centres are not located in separate areas but integrated into the urban grain.

Rather than demolishing the military buildings, these were instead rapidly and flexibly converted for new uses. Workshops and student accommodation, exclusive lofts and communal housing projects moved into the old buildings. These form the backbone around which the new quarters have grown, which with a density of between 200 and 300 persons/hectare are more akin to a turn-of-the-century neighbourhood than the average new housing estate. Although this level of density is not without its concerns, it has tangible advantages: urban spaces are created, many facilities are available close to one another and are only a short distance away, and land prices are affordable for people with average earnings.

Laissez-faire: building cooperatives and land parcelling

The new urban blocks were subdivided much like a large cake: rather than predefining the size of the plots, the blocks were divided according to the appetite of the clients – sometimes they are 4 metres wide, sometimes half a street long. The plots were marketed by the city and sold primarily to private building cooperatives and only rarely to developers. The building co-

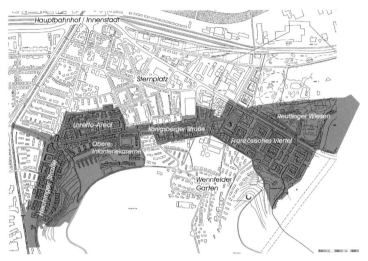

Outline plan for the Südtstadt development, Tübingen.

operatives consist of a group of private persons who cooperate to realise larger or smaller building projects where they retain control of costs, concept and architecture. This has four key benefits for the clients as well as for the city:

- Combination effects for various factors bring cost savings of 15 to 20%; a considerable amount without which many would not be able to afford to build in Tübingen.
- Responsibility for one's own project leads to greater identification with the quarter as a whole.
- As the concept of the building cooperative became more established in recent years, so too

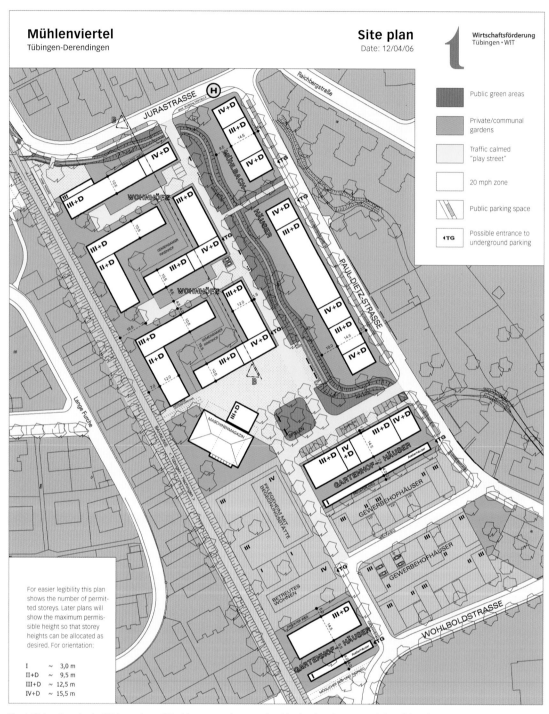

The Mühlen Quarter in Tübingen benefitted from experience gained in the development of the Südstadt.

has the spectrum of different projects. A fundamental process of evolution came about with individual projects developing their own specialisation and niche areas: energy-efficient projects, low-budget houses, a community-oriented group, an intra-generational concept, an architecturally ambitious project, a small project with just two units – the list is long and continues to grow. These all stand cheek by jowl in the same quarter, creating contrast and the desired diversity of concepts, ways of life and building typologies.

■ The breadth and variety of approaches contributes to the fourth advantage: building cooperatives by nature attract a broader range of social backgrounds. For some who cannot afford a developer-built flat or family house, it offers a means to an own home; for others a means of being able to define how they want to live themselves. Many people who could have afforded a house in the periphery were attracted to the idea of a building cooperative as a means of enjoying the urban atmosphere of a dense and mixed neighbourhood while being able to influence their own surroundings.

Building cooperatives in the French Quarter.

The outdoor urban space in the Südstadt assumes particular importance: within more dense and mixed structures, such open spaces are not just recreational areas for children and adults but also serve as meeting places for the urban community. Their function as a road or parking area is secondary as parking blocks are arranged at the edge of the quarter. As a result the streets and squares assume the character of "living rooms for the neighbourhood."

Night-time view of the Lorettoplatz.

The former stables in the French Quarter.

Talked about and highly regarded: the collaboration between municipality and private initiatives

The combination of these four elements and the small-scale focus have transformed a series of previously unattractive barracks to a lively urban quarter in the space of just ten years. The success of the initiative has attracted international interest: the city of Tübingen and the urban design office Lehen drei in Stuttgart have been awarded the German and European Urban Design Awards and won first prize in the Stern-Stadt competition as well as many other commendations.

Three aspects were commended special importance: the concerted effort to bring about urban structures, the tangible vitality of the resulting quarters and the collaboration between municipal authorities and private initiatives. The city of Tübingen coordinated all developments and established a special project team – the Stadtsanierungsamt or Urban Development Office – responsible for all aspects of development from the master plan to economic development and the awarding and sale of plots.

Ultimately, however, the new Südstadt district was built and designed by the many architects, building cooperatives and private clients who passionately and actively created their "own piece of the city." The new quarters have, therefore, become platforms that demonstrate the variety and vitality of urban society. For the people who live and work there, the urban envir-

Dense, mixed-use, urban: building the city …

… with private building cooperatives.

onment offers a variety of options for living their own independent and flexible way of life.

From the redevelopment of military bases to industrial brownfield sites

The experiences gained from the quarters in the Südstadt were so positive that from 2002 onwards the City of Tübingen began to look for new ways to transfer the development model to other parts of the city and other scenarios. In 2003 the city established a land development company attached to the city council's economic development department. Its task was to acquire industrial brownfield sites, develop an urban development plan in accordance with the city's aims and facilitate their small-scale rede-

velopment. This work was also passed onto the Urban Development Office, which – in addition to its normal duties – took over the role of a private (urban) developer.

The basic principle of this development concept is based on that used for the Südstadt: the city adopts a strong position, not just as the planning authority but also through its land use policy; development is undertaken predominantly by groups of private clients who are given as much freedom as possible; all relevant aspects of the complex development are coordinated by a dedicated office in the local authority.

What makes this development interesting is that the active involvement of the city in real estate development is not restricted to a particular location or legal model, such as a development programme, but can be transferred to fit other situations – providing, of course, that there is the political will. The new quarters benefit from the experience gained in the development of the Südstadt, although not all aspects and building blocks are transferred wholesale. Instead, the different models follow the same governing principle: it is the role of the city to create the conditions for the development of complex neighbourhood concepts and with it to create the basis for a diverse and heterogeneous property market. This approach is based on a clear understanding of the role of the public and private sectors: whenever the city wishes to pursue strategic development aims, the public authority must intervene actively in order to ensure that sufficient options remain available for private initiatives.

Welcome to suburbia – the southern USA

In 2006, I had the opportunity to visit several municipalities in southern USA as part of a three-week travel grant. Three weeks is only long enough to gain a superficial overview of the situation and my observations are therefore not as detailed as my own experience in Tübingen-Südstadt. I was nonetheless able to acquire a lasting impression of an urban model that contrasts sharply with the notion of the European city.

Suburbs as far as the horizon.

I visited three local authorities, one each in Florida, Arizona and California. Leaving to one side the specific qualities of each city, although interesting, all three places exhibited similar basic characteristics:

- Significant growth with almost unlimited restrictions on land-use;
- strict functional separation between residential and commercial areas;
- development is undertaken by large developer consortia;
- almost no typological variety in residential areas, just single family houses next to one another;
- no noteworthy social diversity as a result of the monotonous typology: the kind of clientele who need and are able to afford 300-square-

Row after row: suburban reality.

metre-large houses with double garage and a large garden do not come from diverse social backgrounds;

■ total lack of recreational and social functions in the public realm: an urban society that is completely reliant on the car as a means of transport and in which shops only function in shopping malls no longer needs public urban spaces;

■ staggering distances: in Riverside in California, a residential area advertises proximity to a public playground as a key location factor. The playground lies just 15 minutes away by car – providing there is no congestion.

Much has already been written about the ecological and economic risks of suburbanisation and we have become uncomfortably aware of how close this system can come to the brink of collapse since the US real estate crisis began in 2008. The subprime mortgage crisis is not just a financial problem but also and specifically the crisis of an urban model and its dramatic lack of flexibility in difficult times.

Equally interesting for me, however, is what consequences this model has for the everyday way of life and activities of individual people and the development of urban society. My time was too short for a more serious inquiry, however, my impressions were sufficient to elaborate some questions:

■ What effect do journey times of two, three or four hours a day have on the quality and vitality of family life? If the next workplace or

Each with its own platform.

Riverside, California.

childcare facility is 20 or 30 kilometres away, what implications does this have when parents wish to take up work again or to work part-time?

■ How robust are suburban structures when biographical crises occur, for example after a separation or the loss of a job? If one can no longer afford to live in one's house or no longer wishes to live together, how far away from home must one move to find alternative affordable living accommodation?

■ What implications are there for society when families with high incomes, families with average incomes and the elderly no longer live in the same neighbourhood? Where do those people live who do not correspond to the archetypal "family with two children?" Do all homosexuals have to move to San Francisco and all seniors to Sun City?

■ Where do people get to know each other when the only remaining primary points of interaction are the school, the church, and the shopping mall?

Obviously, the suburban structures of southern USA are not representative for the multiplicity of urban constellations in the USA. Nevertheless, a key impression remains: as suburbanisation increases, the options open to the individual become more restricted and with it the degree of social heterogeneity.

The former French military magazine in the Loretto Quarter: acquired and converted by a group of private clients.

Access for all: the privilege of the city

What expectations can and should we have of the city today? Perhaps more than anything else, that the city should fulfil the great urban promise of being able to offer its residents a wide variety of different options. This is without doubt the primary task of urban planning: to guarantee residents access to work, culture, and social facilities in prosperous times as well as during economic crises; to provide a wide variety of housing options so that individuals can change their living situation according to their circumstances – and not vice versa; and to provide quarters that are more than a mere agglomeration of real estate, quarters that ideally become places in which its residents can determine their own degree of seclusion or involvement and in which the diversity of modern society can be experienced and yet still offers a modern-day home for everyone. When these are given, there is a good chance that urban structures can form the basis of a pluralist society.

In my view *Access for All* expresses this conception of the city most succinctly. The accessibility and barrier-free nature of urban structures is much more than just a matter of barrier-free access to the urban environment. *Access for All* stands for the design of urban environments that improve the options open to the individual, that enable one to take part in society and provide – in passing as well as on the doorstep – access to the resources that one needs in order to live one's life independently.

I am convinced that this understanding of the city leads to a whole catalogue of practical questions which today's urban structures need to address:

■ What opportunities do children have to independently explore and discover new spaces,

View of the French Quarter.

Aerial view of the Loretto Quarter.

to experience diversity in their local environment and to learn from their own experiences?

- What possibilities do mothers and fathers have to coordinate work and bringing up their children without overburdening themselves on a daily basis?
- What employment opportunities are available for unemployed people in their local environment and how easy is it to come by?
- What opportunities do migrants have to contribute to society and retain their dignity?
- What opportunities are there for older people to meet other generations that are not part of their own family?
- How can today's pluralistic society experience and continually reform itself on an everyday basis outside of rigid institutions?

- What possibilities do individuals have should their personal, social or economic circumstances change radically?

Many of these are without doubt aspects that exceed the scope of urban design itself – and yet urban structures have a particular role to play in society in that they offer as well as obstruct opportunities. Especially when we consider the realities of suburban structures it appears that the supposedly obsolete model of the "European city" can indeed offer a structural basis for actual and wide-ranging *Access for All*.

....

For further information see:
www.tuebingen.de

Syntax –
Planning urban accessibility
Anna Rose / Tim Stonor

From policy to practice – *Space Syntax* evidence-based tools for accessibility planning

Over the last decades we have seen a shift of the UK planning culture from modernist zoning law to spatial accessibility planning policy. This has far-reaching consequences including the requirement of a completely new set of skills for planners, urban designers, and everyone involved in the development process. As a result of this process, there is a real need for the profession to catch up with the changes in thinking and radically adapt the ways of working in order to produce more convincing results. This would support the intentions of policy makers who intend to put all new housing within easy reach of work, education, shopping and leisure facilities. This also requires stronger cross disciplinary integration of the relevant professions, including planning, transportation and economics. In this context, Space Syntax is supporting local authorities and private sector clients in creating a spatial evidence-base for decision taking and in communicating the impact of planning decisions. This article provides background on how the *Space Syntax* method has evolved alongside and in response to developments within the UK planning culture.

The term accessibility

Accessibility describes the degree to which a location or a service is accessible to all its possible users. This captures the availability of transport, access to services and goods as well as access to the means of social and economic participation in a community. On the other hand, the term Universal Access is used to describe a set of design principles that prevent designers creating physical barriers in our built environment on a more local scale. This supports the inclusion of people with any kinds of disabilities within the larger community.

Relating urban form to urban function, Space Syntax is interested in how all different scales of accessibility overlap, thereby shaping our great cities and neighbourhoods into successful communities. Through investigations of urban layout in relation to different scales of movement (local micro environment, neighbourhood, city, region) we can identify how cities are shaping the emerging collective patterns of human behaviour. Great cities provide an environment that is convenient to use on all scales, safe to inhabit and that offers a high choice of lifestyles and economic prospects to a majority of its users. Space Syntax promotes a scientific approach to the understanding of accessibility, which helps contribute to the development of sustainable communities and the long-term value of the built urban fabric.

Through over 20 years of research-informed consulting, Space Syntax has developed a technology that demonstrates the key role of spatial layout in shaping patterns of movement on foot, on cycles and in vehicles. This includes activities such as way finding and purchasing in retail environments, and deals with issues such as social surveillance and vulnerability to criminal activity in buildings and urban settings, and co-presence and communications in the workplace. These findings have been shaping thinking in the planning debate over the last decades in the UK and elsewhere. *Space Syntax* is now an established tool which uses topological network models to understand the impact of modern city planning on communities, and helps to re-shape them. This method is applied to the redevelopment of urban centres and public spaces, the development of spatial strategies for whole cities, and to the regeneration of informal settlements. It allows us to anticipate the success or failure of urban policy in advance of its implementation.

Methodology

The important role of spatial accessibility in urban settlements has been extensively documented. It is widely acknowledged that the quality of urban areas is largely shaped by the patterns of pedestrian, cyclist, and vehicular movement. Key results from previous studies using *Space Syntax* methods demonstrate that patterns of movement are, in turn, strongly influenced by the layout of the "movement net-work" – the way that the systems of roads, walkways, squares, and open spaces are joined together.

With the help of Geographic Information Systems (GIS) and bespoke *Space Syntax* software, we can analyse the movement network to quantitatively measure "spatial accessibility". There are different types of spatial accessibility: the first, "metric distance accessibility" relates to the distance a person would have to travel from one place in the network to the other. The second, "spatial integration accessibility" is concerned with the number of changes of direction that such a journey would require. Spatial integration is frequently more important because it measures the complexity of routes within an urban area.

Knowing about the patterns of spatial accessibility is valuable because they help us forecast movement patterns that we cannot observe directly, either because observations are too costly or because the areas in question have not yet been built.

Understanding the "crisis" of modernist urban principles

So-called failing urban areas inhibit accessibility and social and economic inclusion. It can be demonstrated that tragically, the same spatial

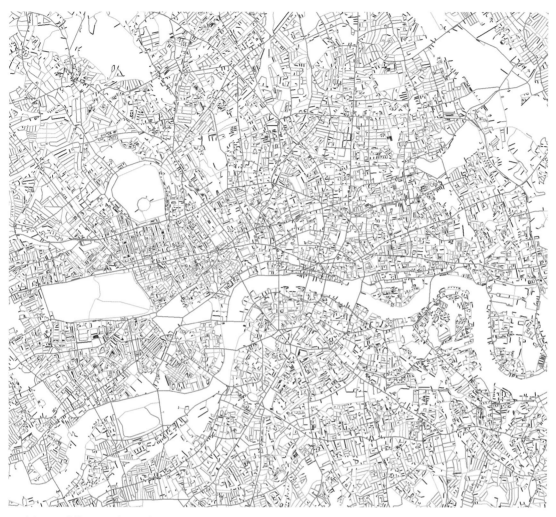

Spatial accessibility map of central London, applying a catchment radius of 10km to each route segment, before calculating its relative accessibility to the overall system.

principles which were originally developed to improve the quality of life of the urban poor at the beginning of the 20th century have significantly contributed to the production of spatially and functionally segregated urban areas with highly unsustainable impacts and high social costs for communities.

The British New Towns have been compared many times with their historic counterparts of similar size. In fact, the concepts of the predecessors of the New Towns, the Garden Cities, were developed by Ebenezer Howard on the notion of a network of small, walkable towns in rural settings. As opposed to their historic counterparts these would be equipped with all the modern amenities such as sewage, electricity, and transport infrastructure connecting them with regional centres. At the time rural towns lacked these amenities and therefore living conditions were poor. Combined with a shortage of jobs in the rural areas, this led to the exodus of the countryside and the overcrowding of the bigger cities.

The initiative of the New Towns as well as a large number of other government housing programmes across the UK and Europe was a reaction to the destruction following World War II, and to the bad state of the so-called inner-city slums. The separation of the different urban functions such as housing, working, industry, and leisure applied in the New Towns has to be understood in this historical and cultural context. At the same time the revolution of private motorised traffic and the negative effect it had on the available transport infrastructure, led planners and politicians to search for new urban models. The famous and influential report *Traffic in Towns* (1963) warned of this effect and introduced a catalogue of measures for traffic management, including the strong separation of cars and pedestrians which today is still influencing the appearance and functionality of modern cities around the world.

New Towns versus evolved cities

In the context of the current tight housing market, the historically evolved cities are generally more popular and achieve higher land values than New Towns of a similar size. Historic centres are seen to be attractive and economically sustainable places worth investing in. Unfortunately, this is not the case for most New Towns. While today both New Towns and historically evolved cities provide the same basic access to modern infrastructure and offer the same quality of transport links to the surrounding region, research by *Regeneration and Renewal* magazine shows that in 2004 three quarters of the 20 New Towns in the UK were among the 50% most deprived UK Local Authorities. Even more worryingly, all but two are more deprived than all the other authorities within their county.

Identifying the difference

Over the last decade Space Syntax has conducted a series of projects that investigate the differences in the urban structure of New Towns and historically evolved cities. We use the term urban structure to define a number of tangible spatial measures which we know have a combined impact on urban activity patterns and the social-economic development of cities. These factors, which influence urban movement, are:

1. Spatial structure,
2. urban block size,
3. land use structure,
4. distribution of population density.

Our studies have demonstrated that historically evolved settlements have certain spatial characteristics in common. It is also important to highlight that their age is a proof of their sustainability, since it highlights their adaptability to changing needs. In most of these cities, the most spatially integrated parts correspond with the centre. There is an accessibility core with a fine urban block structure supporting a mixed-use land use structure which offers short routes between destinations, attracting pedestrians to the area. Within this core we also find all major transport interchanges and regional functions, which are concentrated along the main movement corridors. This type of city supports a mixture of transport modes.

The "New Towns Act" 1946 initiated the development of satellite towns within commuting distance of existing cities. They were supposed to offer mixed-use communities for living and working. Many studies show that this mixture could not be sustained as planned and that most of the town centres in the New Towns have not succeeded economically. In a typical New Town the accessibility core does not necessary overlap with the functional core of the town centre. In that sense, the spatial pattern does not reflect the distribution of the hierarchy of the main functions. Highly integrated segments of the route network are usually reserved for one mode of transport, most often for vehicular traffic. As a consequence, New Towns create extremely spatially segregated networks which are hard to navigate for pedestrians. This leads to low levels of co-presence and social surveillance which has a direct impact on character and feelings of security or vulnerability. These issues have a significant influence on the social and economic profile of these cities. Pedestrian data of eight evolved cities and five New Towns of comparable size highlight significantly lower quotas of pedestrians in the New Towns, which reflects unsustainable transport behaviour.

Sustainable communities and accessibility planning

During the last decades of the 20th century, a new Labour Government in the UK faced two major challenges: regeneration of failed modernist

Syntactic patterns of two towns

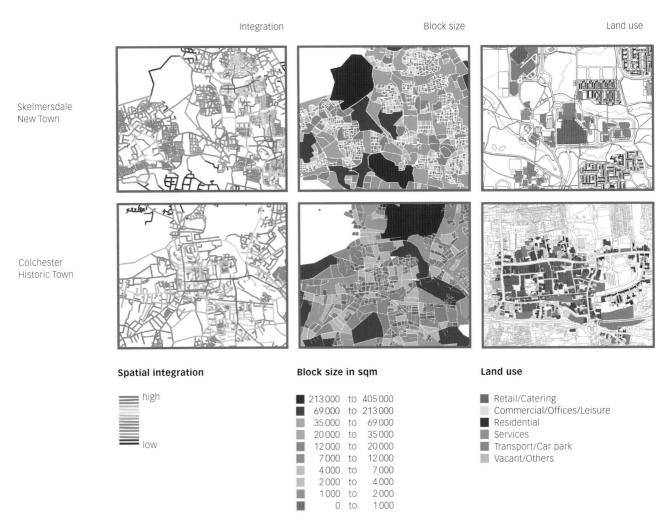

Integration   Block size   Land use

Skelmersdale
New Town

Colchester
Historic Town

Spatial integration

≡ high

≡ low

Block size in sqm

■	213000	to	405000
■	69000	to	213000
■	35000	to	69000
■	20000	to	35000
■	12000	to	20000
■	7000	to	12000
■	4000	to	7000
■	2000	to	4000
■	1000	to	2000
■	0	to	1000

Land use

■ Retail/Catering
□ Commercial/Offices/Leisure
■ Residential
■ Services
■ Transport/Car park
▨ Vacant/Others

Syntactic comparison between Skelmersdale New Town and Colchester, a historically evolved city.

areas and the development of new housing to accommodate growth in demand. The report *Towards an Urban Renaissance* written by the new urban task force under Lord Richard Rogers deals with the question of how to build 4 million dwellings within the next 25 years without making the same mistakes of post-war urbanism and without destroying too much valuable landscape.

Apart from proposals to relax planning laws on density and parking requirements, recycling of brownfield sites and promotion of public transport, the report demands fundamental changes to the planning system in the UK. The Sustainable Communities Plan defines areas for growth predominantly within the industrial belt in the north of the country and the Thames Gateway.

The report *Making the Connections* (2003), published by the Social Exclusion Unit in 2003 is triggering far-reaching reforms in the planning system. Accessibility planning will replace many of the existing planning instruments and local strategies should guarantee that communities are planned holistically so that all relevant functions (education, workplaces, retail, health facilities, child care, culture, and leisure) can be accessed easily on foot and by public transport. Planners are now responsible for wide ranging aspects of public transport as well as for the spatial organisation of different uses and planning for sustainable transport strategies.

The British planning system builds on a negotiation process between all stakeholders. Therefore, clear guidance and requirements are necessary for a successful planning process. Developers are well advised to produce the evidence to prove compliance with local and national planning policies. The official national guidance documents *By Design* and *Safer Places* promote high standards in urban design and provide best practice advice. However, the principles promoted in *By Design* are not always easy to evaluate objectively. While most stakeholders agree with the stated aims, few tools are available for evaluating design proposals against them. In 1999, the government founded CABE (Commission for Architecture and the Built Environment) to serve as a "government watchdog" for design quality. CABE advises public and private sector agencies, organises design review panels, promotes education projects and carries out extensive research in the fields of architecture and planning. CABE's housing audit in 2006, evaluated 100 new residential developments which had been built between 2003 and 2006 and concluded that only 18% of all projects could be classed as good or very good. Too many of the developments did not reach the standards stated in *By Design* and other best practice

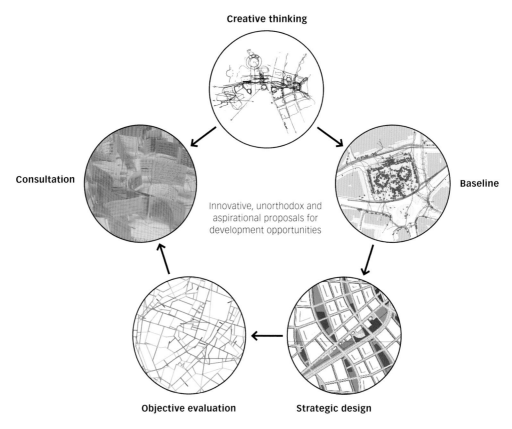

Creative thinking

Innovative, unorthodox and
aspirational proposals for
development opportunities

Consultation

Baseline

Objective evaluation

Strategic design

Evidence-based design process, as developed by Space Syntax.

documents and most problems were identified in suburban areas. They also concluded that new housing, mostly without character, provided a low quality pedestrian environment and the needs of the car superseded the needs of the pedestrian in the public realm landscape.

Evidence-based creativity

In supporting clients in understanding and controlling the impact of spatial layout in any development, Space Syntax developed a set of evidence-based processes and tools which can be integrated in the creative design development process. The use of the *Space Syntax* methodology adds value in the following three stages:

1. Diagnosis: measuring spatial potentials and constraints of an area is the first step towards the identification of new opportunities in any area.
2. Prognosis: design evaluation and optimisation tools give reassurance when a design is

developing in a favourable way or alert the team when it is in danger of functional failure.

3. Communication: *Space Syntax* methods allow us to speak a common, spatial language that cuts across disciplinary boundaries and translates the objectives of planners, designers, transport engineers, economists, developers, investors, and members of the public in such a way that they can be understood by all and organised into meaningful, practical frameworks for action.

....

Further reading and selected websites

Bill Hillier and Julienne Hanson, *The Social Logic of Space*, Cambridge 1984.

Bill Hillier, *Space is the Machine*, Cambridge 1996.

B. Hillier, A. Penn, J. Hanson, T. Grajewski and J. Xu, "Natural movement: or, configuration and attraction in urban pedestrian movement", in: *Environment and Planning B*, no. 20, 1993, pp. 29–66.

Department of the Environment, Transport and the Regions (Ed.), *Towards an Urban Renaissance*, London 1999.

Department of the Environment, Transport and the Regions (Ed.), *By Design*, London 2000.

Peter Hall and Ebenezer Howard, *To-morrow. A Peaceful Path to Reform*, London 2003.

Joey Gardiner, *Regeneration and Renewal Magazine,* London 2004.

A. Rose, C. Schwander, C. Czerkauer, R. Davidel, "Space Matters, Regelbasiertes Entwerfen: Pattern, Graphentheorie", in: *ARCH+*, no. 189, 2008, pp. 32–37.

www.spacesyntax.com

www.spacesyntax.org

www.cabe.org.uk

www.academyofurbanism.org.uk

www.communities.gov.uk

Jeddah Strategic Planning Framework

Background

Space Syntax was commissioned by the Municipality of Jeddah to create a spatial development strategy for the city. Working closely with the Municipality we have built an evidence-based development strategy and produced a set of urban design guidelines. The project covered three potential growth scenarios for the whole city and proposals for a number of action areas.

One of the key aims of the project was to rebalance the growth of the city to the north by strengthening the city centre and its immediate surroundings. This was achieved by promoting strategic new developments within the old airport site, the central waterfront area, and in the unplanned areas surrounding the city centre.

Challenges

The most challenging aspect of this project was the sheer complexity of the social, cultural, economic, and environmental issues that had to be integrated in the planning process. Jeddah's population is extremely diverse, hosting migrant communities from the entire Muslim world, as well as the strong Arabian host culture. Many migrants are extremely poor, living in desperate conditions in older buildings or unplanned developments, which on the other hand form the basis of the livelihood and local econo-

Jeddah's historic core.

my of a large number of residents. In order for Jeddah to realise its potential and benefit from the cultural and social diversity of its population, it is essential that the poorer and more affluent segments of the community, and the different ethnic groups be brought together into an inclusive society. The spatial structure of the urban landscape is possibly the most important mechanism at the disposal of planners seeking to achieve these objectives.

Solution

Space Syntax analysis techniques were used first as a diagnostic tool to understand how the history and evolution of the city's structure has led to patterns of density, land use, and socio-economic settlement. The spatial causes of what

are seen as barriers to social cohesion were identified and a priority list of objectives for the masterplan was drawn up.

Next, the analysis was turned into an option appraisal to allow different spatial strategies to be tested and their likely impacts measured. A spatial strategy and a development density strategy were defined for the whole city, including its peripheral development areas and detailed urban design guidelines were defined for each development area. The strategic planning framework was adopted by the Municipality of Jeddah in 2006 and is part of the emerging Jeddah Plan.

Combined spatial and land use measures highlight the shift of town centre activity to the north.

Jeddah Central Urban Area Masterplan

Concept masterplan and urban design guidelines

On the basis of our work with the Municipality, the waterfront area was identified as one of several strategic development zones to support the regeneration of the city centre. Space Syntax led a concept masterplan for the regeneration and development of a 500-hectare part of Jeddah city centre, with Abdulaziz Kamel Consulting Bureau and Arup for Urban Development Co. Ltd. This is a very challenging area of central Jeddah, where the historic core, waterfront, unplanned areas, and major arteries of the city meet.

The design concept proposes a permeable zone along the whole of the waterfront area, including public facilities such as parks and promenades, restaurants and cafés. Vehicular traffic will be organised around the historic core of the city, while all other routes prioritise pedestrians, public transport, and service vehicles. This system will be connected to existing and proposed new radial routes through the surroundings of the historic core. The design of these routes will provide the highest possible standards of pedestrian amenity, while building mass and landscape

Degree of accessibility to major services

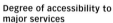

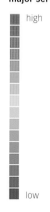

high

low

Degree of
accessibility

high

low

Growth development scenarios of Jeddah.

left: existing, middle: current plan, right: promoting regeneration of the city centre (Space Syntax proposal)

Spatial strategies and land use planning for the ring of unplanned areas surrounding the historic core of Jeddah.

are used to modify the micro-climate via strategic green east-west corridors. Radial routes will
allow city core activity to diffuse into surrounding neighbourhoods. A continuation of the pedestrian environments of the historic Souqs,
Nada and Qabil, will provide additional shopping, tourism and leisure opportunities in a
comfortable environment, whilst significantly
contributing to employment and the local eco-
nomy.

The highest potential for regeneration is
identified around the lagoons and the development areas near the historic core and the proposed Shoreline Park. This area has been assigned to Urban Development Company, which
is leading a local land owner consortium. Space
Syntax is assisting this consortium in preparing
design guidelines for a comprehensive master-

plan proposal, which is currently developed by
a high profile, multidisciplinary team of international designers and engineers.

Growth strategy and local sub-centre development.

Concept masterplan central urban area.

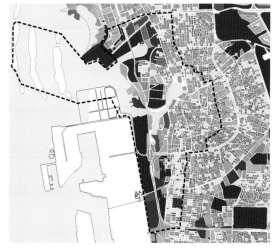

Existing block size.

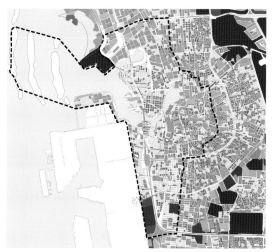

Proposed block size.

Spatial analysis of the existing town centre and pedestrian movement modelling of design options.

Skelmersdale Town Centre, UK Masterplan Development

Background
Space Syntax has been involved in an advisory role in the design and development of Skelmersdale Town Centre. Space Syntax tested the Benoy Architects masterplan and appraised various design options which were then progressed in stakeholder workshops in July and September 2007.

Challenges
Currently Skelmersdale suffers from a number of spatial problems typically associated with New Towns:

- no overlap between different scales or modes of movement,
- two distinct movement networks for pedestrians and vehicles,
- a number of clusters of over permeable, single-use housing estates located away from the town centre and connected back to it (and other estates) very poorly (bottom left),
- a town centre composed of very large, inward facing and impenetrable blocks, isolated from its surroundings.

These spatial problems can result in increased car use, increased levels of crime, and economic

problems such as low property values and a reduced retail concentration.

Solution
The masterplan as shown begins to address
these problems and makes a number of positive
contributions to the spatial structure which include:

- overlaps between the different scales of
  movement, each of which strengthen the
  town centre,
- the global structure of the town centre is
  based around the primary and secondary network of streets instead of the network of pedestrian paths at present,
- the town centre is defined at the local scale
  for the first time and begins to link the south-
  east with the north-west, the focus of the
  vehicular model shifts from dual carriage-
  ways to include the high street.

The masterplan proposal illustrated here shows
the extent of intervention in the centre. The
main route alignments create a direct north-
south connection through the town that accom-
modates both pedestrian and vehicular movement and an east-west connection straight
through the lower level of the concourse, past
the Asda Supermarket and onto residential
communities at either end. Non-residential ac-

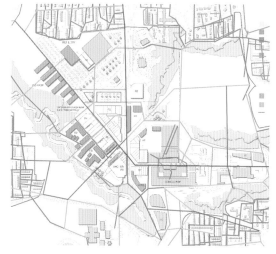

Degree of accessibility

high

low

Detail of pedestrian movement model of the proposed masterplan for Skelmersdale town centre.

tivity is then placed along these strategic connections to pick up on the natural movement
along them. The college is situated to the north-
west of the site, near the town centre but away
from the highest movement rates associated
with retail and the major route intersections.

The masterplan was adopted as a supplementary planning document in September
2008.

Image –
The imaginary as an instrument of urban and regional planning
Wolfgang Christ

L.A. 70 times over

For a brief period in 1984, the people of Los Angeles were able to experience a new, unexpected and for many clearly enjoyable sense of identity: they were citizens of one and the same city. It should be noted, that this is by no means self-evident for a city such as Los Angeles. As Raymond Cartier, the French journalist and co-founder of the magazine *Paris Match*, famously proclaimed back in the 1950s, "Los Angeles is so to speak a conglomeration of suburbs waiting for a centre"[1] – a verdict that holds true to the present day. No other city in the world – rightly or wrongly – is, as a product of being omnipresent in audiovisual media, film, television and computer games, so deeply anchored in global consciousness as a prototype of the boundless and centreless megalopolis.

In the summer of 1984, this image shifted and for a short while one was suddenly aware of Los Angeles as a city – in the media, of course, but also in real life. The occasion was the 23rd Olympic Games which were to take place within a radius of 100 miles. As the first privately-financed Olympic Games, the budget was dictated by economic concerns. Existing facilities were renovated, converted, extended. New facilities were conceived from the outset with a view to their later use after the Olympics, or were erected as temporary structures that could

1984 Olympic Games in Los Angeles: *You are here*.

be easily and economically removed afterwards. All in all, not the best possible conditions for creating a coherent impression and presenting an illustrious image to the nation and the rest of the world – or to the "western" world at least, as the "east" boycotted the games.

Nonetheless, it is the visual appearance of the 1984 Olympics that springs most readily to mind. The architect Jon Jerde and his office The Jerde Partnership together with the graphic design office Sussman/Prezja were responsible for creating this image. Under Jerde's leadership, they developed a set of experimental urban building blocks. A series of rules were formulated for using and combining the variety of different standardised elements and 30 different architectural and design teams were then com-

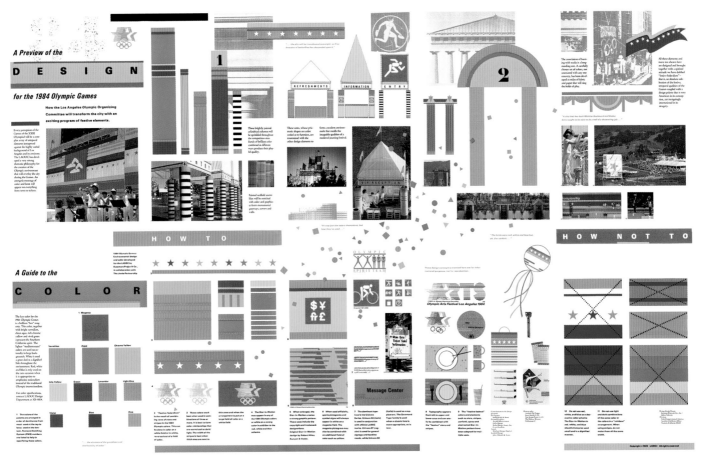

Kit of parts: pages from the design catalogue for the visual identity of the 1984 Olympic Games in Los Angeles.

missioned to implement these for the 70 different Olympic locations dispersed throughout the urban region. With the help of these colourful and expressive, delicate and airy, mobile objects it was possible to create crystallised archetypal images of the south Californian urban landscape which served, for example, as route markers along routes to the Olympic locations, to mark boundaries and entrances, enclose paths and spaces, present information or services or quite simply to decorate buildings and create an artificial urban scenery.

Jerde's low-budget urban design concept[2] sensitively mirrored the self-image of the city: Los Angeles is cosmopolitan, forward-looking, optimistic, lively, fast-moving, colourful and, not least, omnipresent in the visual media. The temporary installations, designed and built using simple, off-the-shelf materials, interpreted

1   Raymond Cartier, *50 mal Amerika*, Munich 1954, p. 63.
2   Frances Anderton, "Urban Transformations", in: Ray Bradbury (ed.): *You are here*, London 1999, pp. 26–33.
3   Gernot Böhme, *Anmutungen. Über das Atmosphärische*, Ostfildern 1998.
4   Gernot Böhme, loc. cit., p. 55.
5   Gernot Böhme, loc. cit., p. 70.
6   Wolfgang Christ: "Stadttyp Europäische Stadt", in: K.-W. Schulte (ed.), *Immobilienökonomie*, Band III: *Stadtplanerische Grundlagen*, Munich 2005, pp. 365–412.

the spirit of the city in a manner of their own. They offered the people of Los Angeles – an exceptionally ethnically, culturally and socially diverse as well as geographically segregated society – something with which they could all identify. Consequently, the Olympic locations told a story for everyone. They created places of common identity. The resulting visual network of landmarks and their presence, both in the urban environment as well as in the urban media, helped condense a 1000 square kilometre city of labyrinthine complexity into a comprehensible urban figure that everyone could relate to.

Seen today, some 25 years later, the architectural interventions for the summer Olympics in Los Angeles seem like a fortunate product of an experiment in an urban laboratory charged with ascertaining how residents can feel part of the urban society of today's vast cities, metropolitan regions and megacities; to find out where they can meet; what communal experiences they share and what common imagery they respond to both consciously and subconsciously. In short: the challenge of how, as an individual, one can relate to urban surroundings that are subjectively perceived as being endless.

Reproducing the image of a city seventy times over makes us aware of two phenomena:

firstly, a city must provide places that invite one to engage with it; secondly, these places need to communicate an impression that people respond to, or speak a language that is understood by as many people as possible. This offers the chance of developing a relationship founded on what Gernot Böhme terms the medium of "atmosphere."[3] In contrast to the image, which is a "consciously outwardly expressed image of itself, or rather the totality of the preconceptions which those outside of the city have of it,"[4] "the atmosphere of a city is the subjective experience of the urban reality which the people in the city share with one another. They experience it as something objective, as a quality of the city."[5]

Foam City

When we think of the image of a traditional European city, it is easy to picture a city that is embedded in a characteristic landscape, whose regional building tradition relates the stories of individual houses, whose public spaces reflect self-assured citizenship and which testifies overall to the events of many hundreds of years.[6] In both a literal as well as metaphorical sense, it builds numerous bridges which enable us to enter into a relationship with it – whether as a tourist or resident. In the "city of old," this prin-

The yearning for a sense of centre: Piazza del Popolo, Rome.   Allianz Arena, Munich.

ciple of access was cultivated in the design of the public realm. We all know, for example, how city gates and towers mark the point at which we cross the threshold between outside and inside; how avenues and parks facilitate the transition between culture and nature; how market and town squares denote places for commerce and culture; and how church and cemetery mark the transition between the earth and heaven. Here, access is not achieved through levelling the transition between different profiles but in fact the very opposite: the more distinct the profile of the places, objects or milieu to be connected, the more striking the moment of access becomes and the more demonstrative its architectural expression in the urban realm.

At the larger scale of the urban region, we rarely experience any of this. Here, urban dichotomies have all but dissolved. *Zwischenstadt*, the city in-between, is everywhere.[7] Nevertheless, in Europe and in the USA, a sense of connection with place still serves as a means of engendering a sense of responsibility[8]: responsibility towards our everyday surroundings, the world in which we live, work and reside, as well as a sense of commitment and responsibility towards the process of urban development when planning and designing our living environment.

For community building at an urban level, the sheer size of metropolitan regions and megacities represents a barrier that for most people

7   Thomas Sieverts, *Cities without Cities. An Interpretation of the Zwischenstadt*, London, New York 2003.

8   Harald Bodenschatz, Barbara Schönig, *Smart Growth – New Urbanism – Liveable Communities. Programm und Praxis der Anti-Sprawl-Bewegung in den USA*, Wuppertal 2004.

9   Peter Sloterdijk, *Sphären III. Schäume*, Frankfurt 2004, p. 626.

10 Wolfgang Christ, Lars Bölling, *Bilder einer Zwischenstadt. Ikonografie und Szenografie eines Urbanisierungsprozesses*, Wuppertal 2005.

is hard to overcome. *Being part* of the city is, however, the basis for *taking part* in the city. Similarly, being able to communicate, to *impart*, is a fundamental experience in engaging with one another, both for the city as well as its citizens. Social networks such as MySpace or Facebook employ the Internet as a kind of virtual small town environment, facilitating face to face contact on screen. Economic networks such as banks or mobile telecommunication companies develop community strategies by "branding" charismatic places in metropolitan regions and cities. Given the relative anonymity of the market, their aim is to forge a symbolic link between the provider and customer, the network and its users, between technology and people. It is no coincidence that sports stadia and arenas are favourite targets for branding initiatives. Peter Sloterdijk has described these buildings as "the cathedrals of post-Christian society." He uses the metaphor "foam city" to describe an urban landscape without centres, inhabited predominantly by "singles and small families" living in multiple isolated cells next to one another. Such "mass containers" satisfy the inhabitants' yearning for a centre, effectively simulating a sense of centrality for the masses.[9] One of the principal sponsors of the Olympic Games in Los Angeles in 1984 was McDonalds, who made profits of around 200 million dollars.

Pantheon, Rome, 2nd century A.D.: access to the gods in the city.

Cardo and Decumanus

If the city in its original sense can be understood as a place for communal activity, then it is clear that we also need to develop means and ways of engendering civic identification at the scale of the urban region.[10] This includes the founding of a parliament for the urban region which would be responsible, for example, for managing the metropolitan region and making politically important decisions. At the level of urban and regional development, however, this should only concern the urban physical and spatial dimensions of enabling *Access for All*: what original function does medium of space have in this respect? What form, effect and meaning do

Pantheon, Rome: an architecture of access to philosophy, the city and the state.

places that enable access to the city have? Which traditional "bridges", that in the past facilitated access in the "city of old," have the potential to be employed in a contemporary form at a much larger scale? Which methods and instruments of access – appropriate to modern ways of life and technologies – lend themselves particularly well to representation through the media? In short, what unique selling proposition can architecture offer in the context of the debate on access to the city?

The observations outlined here give no clear picture. Rather, access to the city of the 21st century shifts ambivalently between different poles, between authentic atmosphere and orchestrated image, between civil society and community, between real and simulated participation, between *Genius Loci* and branded locations, between city gates and web portals. Idealistic aspirations collide with market requirements. Nevertheless, some initial hypotheses for the design of a strategy for access to urban environments can still be formulated. Firstly, *Access for All* is not a spontaneous or sporadic occurrence but should be based on a network. Secondly, the network and nodes of this system of access need not to be commercially controlled or drawn up by public authorities. Thirdly, built forms of access to the city must assert themselves against the prevailing dominance of economic and private interests in the urban realm.

In the early days of the European city, three places existed that both represented the city as well as facilitated access to the city: the agora as a place for communicating with one another, the temple as a place for communicating with the gods and the necropolis as a place for communicating with the dead. Access to the city acquired a rational structure with the introduction of the urban grid plan by Hippodamus of Miletus. The Greek colonial cities, such as Naples, communicated urban culture in the form of a plan layout. *Cardo* and *Decumanus*, the east–west and north–south axes, define at their point of intersection the centre, the *mundus*, of the Roman city. This point is symbolically linked to the

....

11 Lars Bölling, *Das Bild der Zwischenstadt – Dekodierung und Inszenierung räumlicher Identität als Potenzial zur Qualifizierung der verstädterten Landschaft*, Dissertation, Weimar 2008.
12 James Hume, *Will Alsop's SuperCity*, Manchester 2005.

The development of an urban region: the Rhine-Main area in 1925 and 1990.

planet and the cosmos. The boundary of the city, signified by a furrow in the ground, later by a palisade or massive wall, separated the civilised space within from the wilderness of the natural surroundings beyond. The later dismantling of the city walls and the introduction of technical infrastructure – railways, telegraph lines or drinking water and sewage canalisation – into the then still compact body of the city, marked the beginning of the process of technical and spatial networking of the city with the landscape, the city with the world, and ultimately the physical with the virtual realm.

Over the centuries, the city has been a sphere of radical spatial centrality and concentration. Its systems of access were simultaneously systems of power. They are an expression of the catalogue of the rights and obligations of its citizens, merchants and craftsmen. This influence is clearly visible in the functional and social segregation of the built form and space of the city. Each location has its precise coordinates of access: separate streets for the

trades, different market squares for all manner of different products, churches or monasteries. Gates open and close for the city as a municipality.

SuperCity

The current trend throughout Europe towards the formation of urban and metropolitan regions and urban corridors has ruptured our established image of the city. The city has literally fallen by the wayside. It has all but disappeared from view. Different countries have coined a series of terms such as sprawl, *Zwischenstadt*, *Nevelstad*, *Tussenland* or *Città Diffusa* to describe this phenomenon.[11] Terms such as "urban" corridors and "metropolitan" regions stretch the semantic definition of "the city" beyond recognition. There is no longer a natural analogue in the everyday world for the city of the 21st century: urban corridors extend, for example, along the M62 between the coastal cities of Liverpool and Hull in central England,[12] along the so-called Rhine-

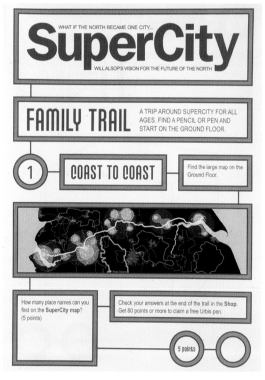

Will Alsop's SuperCity: a playful discovery of the urban region.

perience has shown that they profit from the principle of clustering by mutually attracting other related functions, uses and milieus. They are also the winners in times of demographic change and migration away from shrinking regions and cities. Similarly, they stand to benefit most from the abandonment of the welfare state principle of guaranteeing equivalent living conditions, also in terms of area. The concentration of public and private capital in growth centres will further underpin and strengthen the location factors of the urban corridors.

Metropolitan regions develop, generally speaking, in two different patterns: on the one hand, through the cellular division of classic monocentric metropolitan cities, for example London. In such metropolitan regions, a large number of often very different new centres in the outlying regions grow around the historic centre. On the other, through formal mergers of cities and municipalities to form a larger metropolitan region. They respond to the increasing manifestation of functional zoning which by now also influences the education, culture and recreational sectors with the result that the entire region becomes the everyday environment for its inhabitants. The European metropolitan regions, eleven of which are located in Germany, are of a sufficiently large order of magnitude in operative terms to compete successfully at a

corridor in Germany or between Milan and Venice in northern Italy. The backbone for these band-like urban agglomerations typically consists of clusters of transit and communication infrastructure. In the European Union, these urban corridors are seen as areas of growth. Ex-

....

13 École nationale supérieure d'architecture et de paysage de
     Lille (ed.), *L'espace de la grande échelle/Space on a large
     scale*, Paris 2006.

global level for jobs, investments, residents and tourists.

If we take a closer look at the emerging "large scale"[13] of urban development from the viewpoint of *Access for All*, we can identify three key questions for the future: how can we re-interpret the process of agglomeration of cities in the region as growth of "the city?" Or, does the quality of cities in the traditional sense sink to the same degree as they grow quantitatively? How can urban regions learn from the emanci-patory his-tory of the city in Europe: what spe-cific "urban promise" can they offer? And finally, is the congruence of place, structure and form of the city as a traditional means of engender-ing identity and facilitating access to the city also conceivable at a large scale in the form of a regional figure of the city?

Separation and isolation

The "Ruhr Metropolis" provides an example of how *Access for All* could be achieved in the city of the 21st century. Still known colloquially as the "Ruhrgebiet," the region is comparable with other stretches of land in Europe that experi-enced extensive urbanisation during the period of industrialisation. Three names that have suc-cessively been used to characterise the region – "Ruhrpott," "Emscher Park" and "Ruhrstadt" – tell

The view from the top of the Gasometer in Oberhausen: the infrastructural landscape of the "Ruhrpott."

of its development over time, and of the con-comitant structural changes in the principle of access to the city. To understand this develop-ment in the context of the Ruhr region, one must first picture a region that until the mid 19th century was a typical, predominantly rural, cultural landscape with around half a million inhabitants. From then on a period of incompa-rable growth began. From all over Germany, and from Eastern Europe in particular, people flocked to the region to work in the mining, iron and steel industries. Manufacturing, chemical and energy and power industries followed soon after. As in England, textile industries also played an important role, as we know from the biography of Friedrich Engels who came from a family of industrialists from Wuppertal, which lies on the edge of the Ruhr region. By the turn of the century, the number of inhabitants in the Ruhr region had reached three million. In the 1960s, almost six million people lived and worked in the region. In the year 2000, only six of the 128 mining pits remained, and the workforce had shrunk from 400,000 to only 40,000. Coal extraction had been all but abandoned. Today around 5.4 million inhabitants live within an area of 4,400 square kilometres, which equates to a density of around 2,000 inhabitants per square kilometre, almost ten times the national average. Around 600 kilometres of motorway, 1,470 kilometres of railway lines, 70 railway stations and four airports provide access to a region containing some 300,000 businesses, 16 universities and the world's highest density of theatres, opera houses, concert halls, museums and galleries.

At the height of industrialisation, the Ruhr region was known as the "Ruhrpott": a melting pot of industry, city, landscape and the people who lived there. Access was wholly oriented around extracting and processing raw materials, binding the workforce to the industrial works and supplying the market with massproduced goods. The key aspect of access to the region lay, therefore, in the provision of technical infrastructure. Mechanisation began to take command (Sigfried Giedion). Technical civilisation is founded on supply and disposal systems above ground, at ground level and below ground. The Emscher is a representative example of how a naturally meandering river that crosses the region from the east to the Rhine on the west was transformed into the world's largest network of drainage canalisation. The building of the system of canals was finished in 1906 and channelled waste water from the entire region. Accordingly, the architecture of the Ruhrpott was dominated by structures for technical access, railway lines, embankments, viaducts and bridges, switching towers, freight and public railway stations, railway switching points, winding shafts, gasometers, cooling towers, steelworks and coking plants, piping and cabling for water, gas, electricity and telephone, high-voltage power lines, warehouses and workers' housing estates, roads, trams, waterways and harbours.

During this period the natural habitat disappeared almost entirely. Its aesthetic appearance was consumed along with its raw materials. Moves to resist this development began to be mobilised. Local history and conservation movements, moves to save the remaining intact natural habitat, and restoration initiatives signalled the birth of regional planning in Germany. The *Siedlungsverband Ruhrkohlenbezirk* (SVR), founded back in 1919, designated the first protected green areas as stretches of open corridors

....

14 Technische Universität Dortmund (ed.), *Internationale Bauausstellung Emscher Park. Die Projekte 10 Jahre danach*, Essen 2008.

in the industrial landscape. Urban design too began to embrace the large scale. However, the way in which access to the outdoor envi-ronment, to landscape and areas of natural beauty was facilitated followed the spirit of modernism, which itself stemmed from the industrial age. In order to plan and design each function optimal-ly, functions were separated and zoned. The principle of access became an instrument of drawing boundaries between the new world of the machines and the old world of nature. For one to function perfectly, the other needs to be held at bay. At the small scale, living and work-ing were separated from one another; at the large scale, urbanised industrial zones kept sep-arate from regional green belts. The strategies and architecture of access in the age of modern-ism were, therefore, informed by industrial means of production: serial repetition, mass-reproduction, standardisation and a general emphasis on quantitative values.

Integration and cooperation

The crisis and eventual demise of this epoch led to the establishment at the end of the 1980s of the "Internationale Bauausstellung Emscher Park" (International Building Exhibition). Over a period of ten years from 1989 to 1999, the IBA was a reform agency founded by the state of North-Rhine Westphalia that operated as a think tank for the urban redevelopment of the former industrial landscape.[14] Under its director Karl Ganser, the IBA Emscher Park formed the basis for more than 100 projects and became an international model for urban and regional de-velopment. It showed how industrial heritage could be employed to accelerate modernisation processes and how as a medium for structural transformation, it can become productive in a completely new way.

The name of the building exhibition was itself an outward signal that the impossible has to be made possible if one is to make Germany's industrial heartlands accessible as attractive living and working environments in the 21st cen-tury. Conversion processes with a time span to-talling almost 30 years were initiated to once again transform the Emscher, this time resur-recting it as a river, albeit in a relatively elemen-tary manifestation. The river is the backbone of the Emscher Park, which connects the remain-ing patches of regional green areas diagonally with one another, forming a band that simulta-neously links the cities along the Emscher. The Ruhr region is in reality the Emscher region, en-compassing the larger "Ruhr-Cities" of Duisburg and Essen, Bochum and Dortmund.

The IBA Emscher Park takes the opportu-nity to utilise the vast areas of industrial waste-lands and brownfield sites, along with their of-ten huge structures and open spaces, to establish a new structural network of spaces. Sites that were previously inaccessible, though often centrally-located in the industrial age, are now opened up, effectively removing their barrier-function in the urban landscape and investing them with new uses. The visibility of these structures, for generations closed off behind fences and walls, together with an innovative planning culture has led to the development of new functional and design concepts that illustrate the paradigm shift modernism has undergone. In complete contrast to the early formative period and hey-day of industrialisation, the industrial heritage is now seen as the bearer of a unique potential for developing an individual, unique and local identity, the basis for establishing an emotional bond. Building ensembles originally slated for demolition have become symbols of identity for the region: the Zeche Zollverein in Essen has since been listed as a World Heritage Site for its unique testimony to the architecture of the Bauhaus. The gasometer in Oberhausen has become a venue for spectacular exhibitions and art installations. Slag heaps, immense artificial mountains of stones and constant reminders of the waste material resulting from coal extraction, have become landmarks in the Emscher Park. New residential neighbourhoods and businesses have arisen on brownfield sites. In Duisburg, an entire steelworks embodies the new relationship to indus-

trial heritage, the industrial landscape and the social acceptance it has now attained as a symbol of "home". Factory buildings and workshops have been repurposed as theatre and concert halls or congress and event locations. And a closed network of footpaths and cycle paths now criss-crosses the Emscher region, a new level of infrastructure in the region that, for the first time in modern history, is not associated with work.

The IBA Emscher Park has developed its projects step by step in an ongoing process of discourse as a kind of metropolitan collage of local, independent and self-assured locations. Artists were involved in project developments from an early stage. Competitions were announced to find new concepts. The region has demonstrated an openness to expertise and input from outside. In the process, local qualities and beauty assume an equal role alongside ecological and economic renewal. Tellingly, the master plan for the IBA Emscher Park was only completed at the end of the ten-year project, not at the beginning. The IBA has managed to bring about a new culture of access: the previous modernist strategies of separation and hierarchy have been replaced by principles of integration and cooperation. Instead of securing and demarcating boundaries, barriers are now being removed. The overlaying and intermingling of previously isolated spheres liberates the

....

15 www.Initiative-Ruhrstadt.de/Ruhrstadt-StadtderStaedte
16 G. Willamowski, D. Nellen, M. Bourrée, *Ruhrstadt. Die andere Metropole*, Essen 2000.

metropolitan region from its notoriously cellular rigidity. The IBA motto "Living and working in a park" is emblematic for the structural transformations, joining three previously isolated functions in a single phrase. The revitalisation of the industrial heritage represents an opportunity to link the memory of a time that unites many people in the region biographically with the beginning of a new age which itself cannot provide a band of unity that compares historically with that of industrial labour. This realisation puts the often immense construction and operation costs of the projects into perspective. In this sense the IBA Emscher Park manages to build a bridge between the "Ruhrpott" and the "Ruhrstadt". To use the terminology of accessibility: the IBA makes industrial functions accessible for urban strategies. Without the vision of the "Emscher Park", there would be no notion of a "city made of cities!"[15]

Although in the year 2000, only a year after the official end of the IBA, the municipal association (KVR) published a book entitled *Ruhrstadt. Die andere Metropole*,[16] it took almost ten years for the idea of the Ruhrstadt to assume concrete dimensions in the form of a successful application to become the European Capital City of Culture in 2010. This success has resulted in a growing readiness to use the terms city and region to describe the same thing. As a kind of interim conclusion, we can outline the fol-

Gasometer Oberhausen: a landmark in the IBA Emscher Park.

lowing hypotheses for the design of an urban strategy of access for the urban region: firstly, *Access for all* has a greater chance of success, the more it reflects the historical development of a region and is able to revitalise its historical heritage; secondly, only a culture of integrative and cooperative thought and action has the capacity to overcome barriers; and thirdly, spaces that are intact in the way they are experienced offer the best guarantee for long-term stable access to the urban region.

Romantic rationalism

In the mid 1990s, a large exhibition took place in the gasometer in Oberhausen. With a dia-

Duisburg Nord Landscape Park, landscape architect Peter Latz.

meter of 67 metres and a height of 116 metres, the "piston gas-holder" built in 1929 is a giant legacy of the industrial age. The exhibition entitled *Feuer und Flamme* (Fire and Flame) documented 200 years of the history of the region, as

the subtitle of the exhibition catalogue explains.[17] A review of the exhibition in the *Frankfurter Allgemeine Zeitung*[18] was accompanied by a photo showing a view from above through the steel trusses that support the expansive interior of the gasometer with the caption "Romantic rationalism: view of the exhibition in Oberhausen". The gasometer was scheduled to be demolished on the 13th March 1988. This never happened thanks to the intervention of the IBA Emscher Park. It has managed to establish both a rationale for romanticism as well as instil a romanticism for the rational. As a result, it has been able to revitalise the then stale process of urban and regional planning.

In the mid-17th century in England, "romanticism" and "the romantic" were used to describe the "fanciful" and "rapturous." One hundred years later, Jean-Jacques Rousseau used the term to describe the "thrill" and "enchantment" of the panorama of the Alps. The Romantics saw the poetic side of the world. August Wilhelm Schlegel wrote: "The process of depoeticisation has gone on for long enough; it is about time to once again poeticise air, fire, water and earth."[19] The artists of the Romantic, in their desire to get to the root of things, were fascinated by the mines in the same way that they were fascinated by ruins, by night-time as well as its opposite, light. Caspar David Friedrich painted transpar-

17 U. Borsdorf (Ed.), *Feuer und Flamme – 200 Jahre Ruhrgebiet*, an exhibition in the Gasometer Oberhausen, Essen 1994.

18 "Feuer und Flamme. Erinnerung an die Zeit der 'Großen Industrie'", in: *Frankfurter Allgemeine Zeitung*, August 27, 1994.

19 Eckhart Kleßmann, *Die deutsche Romantik*, Köln 1981, p. 79.

20 Horst Nitschack, *Kritik der ästhetischen Wirklichkeitskonstitution*, Frankfurt a. M. 1976, p. 136; cited in: Rolf Freier, *Der eingeschränkte Blick und die Fenster zur Welt*, Marburg 1984, p. 18 ff.

ent paintings to be viewed illuminated only by a dim light in a darkened room along with musical accompaniment. The proponents of the Romantic were also interested in puppets, in automatons and artificial people. The figures in their novels are constantly on the move in the search for a clear aim that they, however, never reach. The Age of Romanticism is not least about individualism, in extreme cases about loneliness. The places described in novels or depicted in paintings have something unexpected, unpredictable, overwhelming, perhaps also bizarre. They are authentic – in the way the places and spaces of the industrial age are! Today, in the heart of the urban realm, the industrial heritage offers the equivalent of the shadowy forests, icy seas and shady ravines portrayed by the artists of the Romantic before industrialisation set in: a counter-concept to the contemporary environment and prevailing socioeconomic forces. Now that the heavy industry in the Ruhrpott has withdrawn and its fire has been extinguished, nature is returning. If this process is controlled – as it has been in the Duisburg Landscape Park in the IBA Emscher Park – then we are able to experience the simultaneous process of demise and growth, of stasis and dynamism. It becomes possible to watch a place gradually die. That is no small thing in the heart of one of the most densely settled metropolitan regions in Europe.

Tetraeder: a landmark in the IBA Emscher Park as an iconic symbol of the "Ruhrstadt."

Iconic turn

The transformation of the region's industrial heritage in the 1990s, which also encompasses industrial architecture and the increasingly industrialised natural landscape that surrounds it, constitutes a new aesthetic experience of the city – and with it a new way of accessing the city of the 21st century. We can compare this with the aesthetic experience of nature in the 18th century. "In the landscape, the subject becomes constitutive for the object; through it nature has become a form of space that is experienced. Nature as landscape is nature which is no longer subject to the objective laws of nature and has thus been freed from the clutches of direct exploitation; nature which has taken the place

La Tour Eiffel in "Paris Las Vegas," Las Vegas.

of objectified space!"[20] If one replaces the term "nature" with "city" in this sentence, it becomes clear why an aesthetic experience of the city, in the Ruhr region, has only become possible in the post-industrial age. Only the vast numbers of industrial facilities and areas – that part of the city "that has been freed from the clutches

of direct exploitation" – can be romanticised and are accessible for poetic strategies.

The aesthetic renaissance of the demystified machinery of modernism in the form of "elements of urban beauty" comes at a time in which visual media culture, fuelled by digital technology, is rapidly becoming an everyday part of people's lives. With its help, we are learning to perceive polycentric, dynamic, fragmentary structures which will slowly replace the traditional, centrally-oriented perspective of access to the city via city gates (the railway station for example), along a main axis, with a view of the minster or castle to aid orientation. The Ruhrstadt is presented in the media as an architectural collage. Its set pieces are for the most part identical to those "magical places"[21] from the IBA era. From today's point of view, it is hard to imagine how in socio-political terms it was possible to publicly finance such large-scale projects in a so socially unstable region, all the more so when these projects are "fundamentally useless" – as is epitomised by the "Tetraeder" in Bottrop. Roland Barthes argues, however, that it is precisely this quality that explains the mythology of the Eiffel Tower. It "is a condition for the fact that in essence the tower belongs to everyone. Moreover it belongs to each of our imaginations. A fundamental truth, recognised even by law, as a ruling once permitted everyone the right to reproduce the Eiffel tower: its

21 Olaf Kaltenborn, *Magische Orte*, Essen 2003.

22 Roland Barthes, *Der Eiffelturm*, Munich 1970, pp. 77 ff.

23 www.route-industriekultur.de

24 Roland Barthes, loc. cit., pp. 32 – 33.

25 Gottfried Böhm, "Das Paradigma 'Bild'. Die Tragweite der ikonischen Episteme", in: Hans Belting (ed.), *Bilderfragen. Die Bildwissenschaften im Aufbruch*, Munich 2007, p. 80.

image is not protected property. The Eiffel tower is public."[22]

The "Industrial Heritage Trail"[23] can be seen as stepping stones to the right and left of the Emscher that serve as a playful means of *Access for All* to the history and future of the metropolitan region. To use the language of Roland Barthes in his analysis of the Eiffel Tower, their "usefulness [...] is without doubt incontestable, but appears of ridiculously little value compared with the phenomenal potential it offers to the imagination which helps people to *be* in the actual sense of the word."[24] In technical terms, the tower built by the accomplished bridge builder Gustave Eiffel is "just" a vertical bridge, but in symbolic terms he created probably the most powerful means of *Access for All* to a modern metropolis.

An architecture of the imagination appeals to the people's capacity for fantasy. It stimulates images, images that we make, images that come to life within us. This is what unites Jon Jerde's temporary buildings for the Olympic Games in 1984 in Los Angeles and the superfluous buildings in the Ruhrpott as transformed by Karl Ganser's IBA Emscher Park. In this way – according to our final hypothesis – it is possible to reclaim sensory-coded images of a better world for the arsenal of methods and instruments of urban and regional planning. Here they can work their wonders in the space between the individual and society, between place and city. "The power of an image within us is not jaded by contrasting reality. Because man does not have to subordinate himself to the dictate of fact or existing conditions, because he can imagine a way forward where no path seems possible; this is possible thanks to man's forward-looking, inquiring fantasy and power of imagination. Many open questions are initially full of doubt, apparently insurmountable and allow no way forward. The imagination can be a highly productive instrument which ultimately proves its worth in reality. It is that Plus Ultra, that taps our inner capacity for imagination in order to create external images."[25]

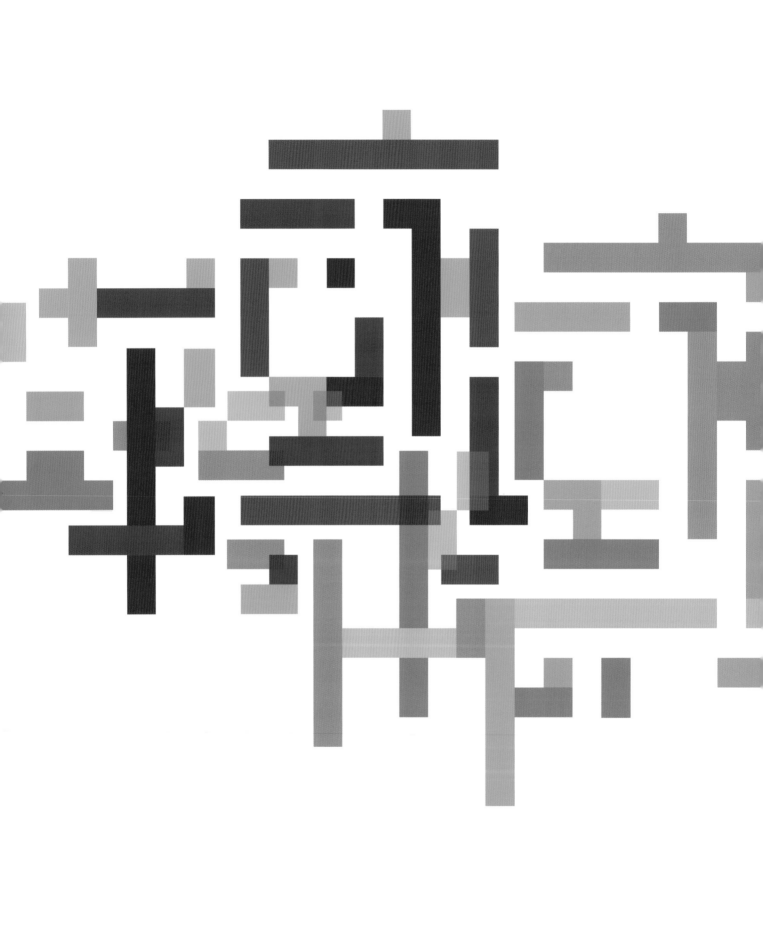

Practice –
Reducing barriers
Susanne Edinger

Less is more

The housing market is awash with all manner of terminology. The elderly in particular, as long-term and reliably paying residents are a much sought-after consumer group, and are courted with promises of *senior-friendly, full-comfort, intra-generational or accessible* housing. Of these, only the term *accessible* is formally defined, and is detailed in the German DIN 18025/2 norm "accessible dwellings." The other "labels" are not obliged to fulfil any meaningful criteria. So how can yet another undefined term, *low-barrier*, contribute to the debate?

The term *low-barrier* aims to relate accessibility targets set down in the building norms to the actual situation in *existing* housing stock. In practice, the adaptation and alteration of existing housing stock to fulfil accessibility norms is beset with difficulties. Passageways may be a few centimetres too narrow, rooms a few square metres too small or the structure or design may prove limiting, for example in the case of historic buildings. It is much more difficult to fulfil accessibility norms in existing housing stock than in newly built housing – and even here it is by no means automatic. Cost constraints are an additional factor. Housing associations and investors are already hard-pressed to provide economical housing at an affordable price for a broad section of society. Accessibility, many be-

Even paving makes it easier to walk or use wheelchairs and strollers in old town centres.

lieve, is often one of the first areas where cost savings can be made. As a result, attempts to reduce existing barriers are all too often abandoned entirely, although a number of measures towards this aim would still be possible.

This is where the term *low-barrier* can contribute. It defines a "collection of measures aimed at reducing barriers in existing dwellings with a view to improving their usability".[1] If it is not possible – or feasible – to adapt housing to fully conform with accessibility norms, then it is nevertheless sensible to remove or avoid as many barriers as possible during adaptation, rather than to ignore the issue entirely.

It follows too that the term *low-barrier* should not be used in conjunction with new housing. Accessibility norms such as the

Because there is no lift, the planners have not considered accessibility needs and in the process introduced new barriers (above): the ramp is too steep, the steps have no handrail and there is an unnecessary step in front of the entrance. In outdoor areas it is much easier to adjust the terrain to avoid the need for steps (below).

DIN 18025/2 apply for all new buildings. The number of new buildings in Germany is, however, relatively small and will remain so in future: while around 200,000 new housing units are built per year, there are nearly 39.5 million existing dwellings. Most of the dwellings in which we will live in the coming decades have therefore already been built. Given ongoing demographic developments, these will also be home to an ever increasing number of older people. Most people wish to continue living in their own four walls for as long as they are able to live independently, and in national terms too this is also the only way to cope with the demand for elderly care as society ages as a whole. The need to make dwellings usable for all sections of society, with particular regard for the needs of the elderly, will in future shift from being a "special needs" consideration to a central principle.

Harmonising everyday usability and design qualities

People's ability to be able to live independently on an everyday basis in their own home, even with physical impairments, is as different as people are themselves. For many residents, even a partial reduction of barriers can substantially improve the usability of their home and their ability to carry out everyday activities. For example:

- For many residents, a lift helps even when one still has to ascend a last flight of stairs to reach one's flat. It is better than having to climb three full storeys.
- It is simpler to manage a single step out onto a balcony than to have to step over a raised threshold.
- A handrail helps residents to ascend or descend even two steps more easily than without such support.
- A door width of 119 centimetres to a bathroom is better than 95 centimetres, even when 1 centimetre short of the 120 centimetres stipulated in the norm.

These are just four examples of the low-barrier adaptation of existing dwellings. More than 80 such individual measures have been compiled in the document *Barrierearm – Realisierung eines neuen Begriffs*.[2] The focus is on small, cost-effective, clever, and practical solutions – exactly the kind of solutions that make it easier for us all to live our everyday lives. This necessitates that planners and architects look closely at how different kinds of people live in their dwellings and living environment, which routes they take, what they change, repurpose or don't use at all.

1   Susanne Edinger, Helmut Lerch, Christine Lentze, *Barrierearm – Realisierung eines neuen Begriffes. Kompendium kostengünstiger Maßnahmen zur Reduzierung und Vermeidung von Barrieren im Wohnungsbestand*, Research project funded by the BBR Federal Office for Building and Regional Planning, issued by the SRH-Hochschule Heidelberg. Fraunhofer IRB-Verlag, Stuttgart, 2007, p. 17.

2   Ibid.

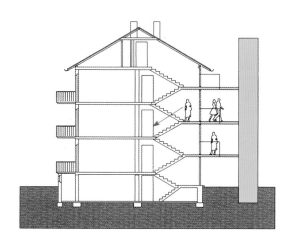

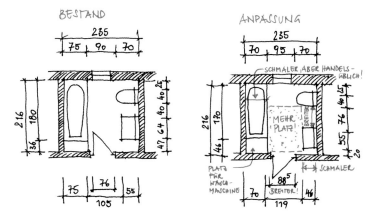

A typical low-barrier adaptation: the lift provides access to each half-landing "only" – an improvement for many despite the need to still use stairs.

Slim-line sanitary installations increase the space available in the bathroom from 105 to 119 centimetres – not quite norm-conform but adequate for most people.

For example, an unused bicycle cellar in an existing building does not necessarily mean that no-one there rides a bicycles. More than anything, it means bicycles first need to be carried up the stairs before one can use them. Residents who find this difficult physically may eventually give up cycling altogether. A simpler and more practical solution is to provide a means of storing bicycles at ground level, for example in the form of individually lockable outdoor boxes. These can also double as a means of providing definition to otherwise open outdoor spaces, for example to help break down the bleakness as-

sociated with high-rise slab blocks and 1950s housing estates. It also helps older people retain their radius of activity for longer and improves everyday life for others as they no longer need to carry groceries and the like all the way home. Similarly, easy access to a bicycle can help people lead a healthier and more enjoyable lifestyle while simultaneously using an ecologically-friendly means of transport.

Another example is the relationship between storage space and balconies: when residents use their balconies as a place to store items from their flat, this suggests that there is

Floor-flush showers should become standard in the future, also for conversion measures. If space allows, partially openable shower cubicle partitions make it easier for helpers to assist.

insufficient storage space in the flat itself. When residents erect screens around their balconies, this testifies to a need to shield against sun, wind and prying eyes which the architecture itself does not fulfil. Maybe the architect minimised the amount of available storage space in the flat to improve the sense of space in the interior; maybe the transparent balcony was intended to communicate a sense of lightness. The architect needs to realise that in such cases the façade may then be dominated by the residents' clutter. Similarly, the residents are forced to cope with an apartment that could have been more usable than it actually is.

What makes architecture both useful and sustainable is its ability to fulfil the needs of its residents while also preserving the planner's design intentions. Good-quality, intelligent solutions of this kind not only help architecture retain its spatial and aesthetic qualities over decades of use; they are also a prerequisite for encouraging long-term residency and identification with one's living environment – which in turn contributes to social and economic stability.

Attention to detail

By striving to achieve the greatest possible reduction of barriers to accessibility, this approach goes further than the conventional interpretation of implementing "specific measures for specific user groups," aiming instead for "universal design" solutions. This corresponds to the definition of accessibility in the norm, which is described as the "capacity of buildings [...] to enable *all people* regardless of age, ability or disability to make largely equal [...] use of its facilities."[3]

The concept of the low-barrier adaptation of existing homes calls on architects, clients, and landlords to examine closely the opportun-

....

3 Draft of the DIN 18030, which is expected to be replaced imminently by the DIN 18040, c.f. http://din18040.de

4 Richtlinien zur Förderung von investiven Maßnahmen im Bestand in Nordrhein-Westfalen (Guidelines for promoting investment measures for existing buildings in North Rhine-Westphalia). Issued by the Federal Ministry for Building and Transport MBV NRW, January 26, 2006, IV B 4-31-03/2006.

ities of removing or reducing existing barriers whenever they undertake works on the building, however small, whether renovation or maintenance work, alterations or conversion measures. At this stage, noticeably improved usability can often be achieved without additional costs. For example:

- The thermostat on a new radiator is positioned so that one can read and operate it when seated.
- A light switch in a retiled bathroom is – compliant with the norm – located at 85 centimetres above floor level so that it can be reached by all users without being uncomfortably low for users who are used to 115 centimetres above floor level.
- A new bath tub is chosen that allows helpers to stand closer to the bath so that it is easier to assist people.

The above examples show clearly that in order to avoid barriers, close attention must be paid to the details of execution when planning building measures. The aim of improving accessibility – whether or not it is 100% achievable – has to inform the entire design process from conception through to detailed planning. By expressly considering such issues in the initial planning stages, one can avoid the need to retrofit special aids at a later date, which are then generally more visually intrusive and announce unequivocally that there are residents who need assistance. Only through such pro-active planning is it possible to achieve more discreet "invisible" accessible solutions that combine usability with elegance.

The fact that the low-barrier adaptation of existing buildings advocates the implementation of measures that do not fully conform to the stipulations of the DIN 18025/2 norm was initially met with some opposition. There were worries that the aims of the norm would be diluted, at a stage when the notion of accessibility had finally gained widespread recognition after nearly 20 years of intensive campaigning. Accessibility as defined in the DIN is now standard practice for new buildings but not for the adaptation of existing housing stock. *Low-barrier* denotes a shift of focus to "achieving as much as possible rather than everything at all costs" and can ease the situation considerably.

This line of thought has now been taken up in the most recent financial aid guidelines[4] and there is growing recognition that a stronger focus on the reduction of barriers to accessibility in existing buildings has a greater chance of widespread implementation so that people can independently live their own lives for as long as possible. Recent German funding programmes

"Discreet" accessibility measures: the topographic situation is cleverly exploited to afford same-level access to the entrance without any steps.

When bicycles can be parked at ground-level, it helps old people in particular to remain mobile for longer.

Facilitating same-level access to balconies eradicates a typical barrier in existing housing stock.

formulate such adaptations as "measures to reducing barriers in existing housing stock," which is a more accurate if wordy description. In Germany the more succinct term *barrierearm* (low-barrier) has, however, quickly become established. Nevertheless, this term unites two words which taken alone have predominantly negative connotations: *barriere* (barrier) and *arm* (weak, poor). A more positive, politically-correct, self-explanatory and easy to remember term with obvious market appeal has yet to be found. The use of Anglicisms such as *Access for All*, although recognised internationally by experts in the field, does not have the same appeal in the German housing market and is more likely to baffle consumers. It seems that a new and more precise term to add to the terminology jungle may be called for. In Germany, two terms currently under discussion are *generationengerecht* (intra-generational) and *demografiefest* (demography-resistent). It will be interesting to see what other proposals may follow and which term will prevail in the long term.

....

Selected websites

www.barrierearm.de
www.susanne-edinger.de
www.irb.fraunhofer.de/bauforschung
www.fh-heidelberg.de
http://din18040.de
www.mbv.nrw.de
www.kfw-foerderbank.de
www.wohnungsanpassung.de
www.mir.brandenburg.de

Everyday life –
Normalisation breeds discrimination
Tobias Reinhard

Longer life expectancy and the increasing problems of old age

Life expectancy in modern, post-industrial societies appears to be growing ever longer thanks to advances in medicine, job legislation, education, and environmental protection. As a result of comprehensive health care, low levels of manual labour, shorter working weeks, and a healthier diet, society is faced with a growing number of pensioners who are no longer in employment but are fit and active and have plenty of leisure time to enjoy.[1] Current demographic changes – in which the "age pyramid" is gradually mutating into an "age pagoda" as the proportion of young people decreases and the number of older people increases – not only present challenges for future pension funding but will also result in an increasing number of older people with physical or sensory impairments who will nevertheless wish to continue to take part in everyday public life.

As studies have shown, longer life expectancy does not result in an extended period of youth but in a significantly longer period of old age. As a consequence, there is a greater risk of suffering from some kind of physical or mental impairment for the last part of our longer lifespan. The following constellations are in principle possible:

- Good mental health but with defective motor functions,
- good physical shape but with defective mental faculties,
- defective motor functions and defective mental faculties.

The ideal scenario, where we remain mentally and physically fit in old age, will increasingly become the exception, despite, or perhaps precisely because of, the great advances made in medicine.

The health hazards of a leisure and pleasure-seeking society

The reduction in the number of workdays per year gives us more time for ever more elaborate and extravagant leisure activities, an increasing number of which are hazardous to our health. Particularly apparent are recreational sports with ever faster sports equipment such as mountain bikes, skateboards or carving skis as well as the growing trend towards extreme sports such as free climbing, paragliding and base jumping, which have resulted in an exponential increase in the number of serious accidents and attendant injuries. Alongside injuries caused by falls, brain damage following diving accidents and chronic disorders sustained as a result of continuous sport-induced strain contribute to a steadily growing number of mostly young sport-invalids who, despite the enormous advances in rehabilitative medicine, will have to cope with restricted independence and an impaired quality of life for the rest of their lives. Long-term social pressures such as unemployment, work-related stress or a lack of perceived prospects, in combination with ever more anonymous leisure activities give rise to a new category of invalids: those suffering from addiction. The burgeoning party scene and wider variety of addictive substances and designer drugs, as well as the widespread availability of medication, contribute to the number of people with long-term health problems stemming from dependency.

Society as a whole is facing new challenges as a result of such developments:

- The proportion of people with disabilities is rising steadily.
- The number of young people with disabilities is growing disproportionately.
- The demands of disabled[2] people in society will rise.
- People with disabilities will no longer be out of the ordinary.
- The unrestricted integration of people with disabilities is a declared aim.

Changing mentality – moving away from the infirmary

A historical review

Society's attitude towards disabled people has changed over the centuries, and more rapidly over the last few decades. Until the Age of Enlightenment, the mortality rate among disabled people was high and disability in general was heavily stigmatised. Those who reached adult age and could not serve any useful purpose in the family were mercilessly cast out of society and were forced to beg to survive. With the Enlightenment, disabled people were gradually accorded more rights. Infirmaries and asylums now served a wider purpose than merely quarantining the sick. Although the establishment of infirmaries improved the social standing of the disabled compared with their previous exclusion from society, housing the disabled in infirmaries did not serve the purpose of integration but rather the structural order of an increasingly rationally organised society. Those who were committed to an infirmary or asylum received a minimal level of care and assistance but were also, to all intents and purposes, "removed" from society. Infirmaries and asylums remained an effective means of segregation which protected the supposedly better society from those who were different. In the 20th cen-

....

1   This is, of course, not universally the case: many teenagers and young adults have unhealthy diets; large sections of the US population have no health insurance; air and water pollution in some industrial regions in China is horrendous, and so on.

2   Despite its widespread use and general understanding, the term "disabled" is not always regarded as appropri-

ate: numerous other, usually cumbersome descriptions or euphemisms are also used in its place but very often entail additional unintended categorisations (e.g. mentally or physically disabled). We prefer to use this unequivocal term in the knowledge that it is usually the inflexible environment or prejudiced mentality of people that actually make people disabled.

tury, such "protective measures" reached their negative culmination with the compulsory sterilisation of disabled people[3] and the euthanasia programmes established by the Nazi regime.

It was not until after the Second World War that previously undisputed "preventative measures" such as compulsory sterilisation, prohibition to marry and other patronising practices were called into question. The right of disabled people to lead a dignified life began to be recognised. Nevertheless, the process of integration progressed only slowly up until the end of the 20th century. Significant improvements in the integration of disabled people first came about as a result of a profound change of mentality among disabled people themselves who were no longer prepared to tolerate discrimination and segregation.

Show booths and vaudeville

Although today unthinkable and degrading, for hundreds of years it was common practice until

Infirmary, 1846.

well into the 19th century to exhibit people with disabilities as a public attraction. As long as the disability was "interesting" and "unique" enough, society seemed willing to forego conventional segregation practices and haul such "specimens" out of the infirmary and into the show booths.

In the 19th century, Joseph Merrick, better known as "The Elephant Man," became famous around the world. He suffered from Proteus Syndrome which disfigured his face and body with grotesque, "elephant-like" tumours and growths. Cast out of society, he earned his living in sideshows and chambers of horrors. He was later given quarters in a hospital by a physician in return for allowing medical examination by medicine students, though even there, patients could pay to see him. Only after direct intervention by Queen Victoria was Joseph Merrick able to live the remaining years of his short life in comparative dignity.

Even in the 20th century, children with conspicuous physical deformations were sold by their parents as a fairground attraction, as was the case with the Siamese twins Daisy and Violet Hilton in 1908. Barely two weeks old, the twins were sold by their mother, who worked as a bar lady, to the lady owner of the bar. From the age of three onwards, the twins began a stage career managed by the bar owner, and their song and dance show travelled throughout England, Germany, Australia and the USA. Aged 15,

....

3   In Switzerland the practice of compulsory sterilisation continued on into the second half of the 20th century.

they were bequeathed to the bar owner's daughter who exploited them for a further nine years. At the age of 24 they finally sued their "managers" and gained their independence. From 1931 to their death in 1969 the twins appeared in their own right in vaudeville theatres in the USA and also starred in a movie.

Public recognition and acceptance

Greater equality for people with disabilities in society was a comparatively late consequence of the Age of Enlightenment and their standing has improved slowly but steadily, although not to the same degree in all cultures. Particular credit should be given to strong-willed and charismatic personalities in prominent public positions who have played a major role in breaking down prejudice and bringing about wider acceptance of people with disabilities. The following personalities stand for all those who have demonstrated endurance, courage and self-confidence in fighting for equal treatment in society and contributed to a general change of mentality over the last 150 years.

The artist Adolf Wölfli, 1864 – 1930

At the age of 26, Adolf Wölfli, farmhand and labourer, first served time in prison after raping a minor. Feeling increasingly lonely, he was again convicted for the same offence five years later and admitted to the Waldau Clinic near Bern as a schizophrenic, where he spent the remaining 35 years of his life. During this period he devoted his time to the production of vast numbers of collages, to writing and creating an epic *Gesamtkunstwerk*. Practically unknown during his lifetime, he was "discovered" in 1945, 15 years after his death, by Jean Dubuffet and is now regarded as a leading exponent of Art Brut and a gifted artist with immense creative energy. In 1950, some 2,000 works by Wölfli, from 45 different collections, were shown at the *Exposition internationale d'art psychopathologique* in Paris, which attracted 10,000 visitors. In 1962, Andy Warhol employed a motif for his iconic Pop Art painting *Campbell Tomato Soup*, which Adolf Wölfli had previously used in 1929 in a collage entitled *Campbell's Tomato Soup*. Is the choice of motif pure chance or is there a link between the beginning of Warhol's career as a graphic artist in 1949 and the Wölfli Exhibition of around the same time? One way or the other, society now pays tribute to the artist Wölfli and accepts his mental and psychological disability.

The politician Franklin D. Roosevelt, 1882 – 1945

At the age of 39, Franklin D. Roosevelt contracted polio and from that point on was confined to a wheelchair. In 1933, after intensive campaigning, he was elected President of the United States of America. Great effort was made to conceal his disability and up until his death in 1945, it was forbidden to publish photographs or drawings depicting the President of the USA in a wheelchair. Even in the first half of the 20th century, therefore, people in the highest positions still felt unable to dispel the stigma of disability; instead, the disability was suppressed and concealed. It was not until 2001, after intensive lobbying by American disability associations, that the unveiling of a bronze sculpture in the Washington Memorial depicting the President seated in a wheelchair publicly acknowledged his disability.

The singer Ray Charles, 1930 – 2004

By the time he was a young man, Ray Charles, blind since childhood, had already overcome numerous prejudices in order to be taken seriously as a musician by the American music business. He went on to become an international star and an icon of soul music. His dark glasses were to become his hallmark. Despite the hard-won recognition he earned, in sixty years of stage appearances he never once appeared without his dark glasses. For the duration of his life, his disability was more or less concealed by a fashion accessory.

The scientist Stephen Hawking, born 1942

Stephen Hawking achieved recognition from an early age. Since childhood he has suffered from amyotrophic lateral sclerosis (or ALS) which results in the degeneration of nerve cells. He nevertheless became a brilliant astrophysicist, expert on black holes and successful writer. Despite seriously incapacitating disabilities he has published numerous pioneering works on astrophysics and quantum mechanics. Since 1985 he has only been able to communicate with the help of a speech synthesiser, selecting each individual word from an on-screen menu by making small hand gestures. He could manage around 15 words per minute, however the progressively degenerative disease has since weakened his hand to such a degree that this is no longer possible. He now chooses words using an infra-red transmitter attached to his glasses which he controls by contracting the muscles in his right cheek. Stephen Hawking continues to publish and is a positive example for people with or without disabilities.

The politician Wolfgang Schäuble, born 1942

The German politician Wolfgang Schäuble is frank and open about his disability. Since surviving an assassination attempt in 1990, he has been confined to a wheelchair but has not withdrawn from politics. He became Home Secretary and was even considered a possible candidate for president of the Federal Republic of Germany. He has not attempted to conceal his disability in any way; the courage and will to pursue his political career is remarkable and exemplary.

The music star Andrea Bocelli, born 1958

Andrea Bocelli was born in 1958 with a hereditary form of glaucoma and his eyesight deteriorated as he grew older. At the age of 12, he lost his sight altogether after a sporting accident. Classical music and singing has been his passion since childhood. Despite his talents he was nevertheless unable to make a living from music and chose instead to study law and worked as a court appointed lawyer. In 1992, after a joint recording with the Italian rock star Zucchero, he finally rose to fame with the title *Con Te Partirò*. Unlike Ray Charles, Andrea Bocelli does not hide his eyes behind dark glasses, whether on stage or in court, and has successfully overcome the stigma surrounding blindness.

Milestones in the development of Non-Government Organisations

The gradual change in public mentality is reflected not only in the lives of prominent people but also in the steadily increasing degree of organised representation among the disabled. Most are in the form of NGOs that represent their interests nationally and internationally and collaborate to form new networks. A number of declarations and action plans for improving the integration of the disabled in society have been issued as a result of their initiatives:

- Founding of the European Institute for Design and Disability (EIDD) in 1993.
- Design for all is propagated as a means of social integration for the disabled.
- In 2002, the Madrid Declaration on Discrimination called for equality for the disabled.
- 2003 was proclaimed the European Year of People with Disabilities.
- In 2004, the Stockholm Declaration was published, introducing the motto *Good design enables, bad design disables.*

Access for All

By the end of the 1990s, the continued lack of public awareness among non-handicapped people for the needs of disabled people along with growing assertiveness and better organisation among the disabled and the availability of technical solutions, led to the formulation of a number of concrete demands by disabled interest groups. These were summarised by the motto *Access for All*.

- Equal access to the urban realm, indoor environments and transport,
- equal access to technical machinery and means of communication,
- equal opportunity to make use of public spaces,
- equal opportunity to take advantage of educational, cultural and other services,
- equal sensory experience for body and spirit.

Alongside these, further mottos were coined:

- Design for all: inclusive design of equipment and spatial concepts,
- smart Architecture for all: buildings and facilities that cater for the needs of people whether disabled or not,
- stimulating environments for all: Natural and urban landscapes that can be experienced by everyone,
- inclusive urbanism: integration rather than segregation; an urban realm for all.

While these mottos adapt, expand, or add focus to the main principle of *Access for All*, the central message remains the same: the need for equality.

Technology in transformation

Alongside a change in awareness in society, an increasing number of technical solutions have been developed specifically for the disabled. There can be no doubt that technical advances and their subsequent application have come about as a direct result of increasing self-assertion and political lobbying by the disabled associations and NGOs. The most visible progress has been made in transport technology, and even more so in communication technology. Improved mobility and specially-adapted communication devices have helped the disabled to expand their radius of action, in turn promoting the development and implementation of ever better assistive technology, a process that reinforces itself in a spiralling pattern.

Greater independence through communication and mobility

A sense of orientation, the ability to perceive dangers, process information, and move around physically are basic prerequisites for today's mobile society. Walking difficulties, poor eyesight, deafness as well as physical disorders or dementia can significantly restrict one's freedom of movement, radius of action and in turn often one's ability to make contact with others.

1975   1995   2005

Thanks to new communication technologies, many of these restrictions are no longer so acute. The widespread availability of mobile telephones has made it possible to conduct conversations from afar and establish networks of contacts. The Internet facilitates the exchange of information as words, images and sound and makes it possible to work without having to be at a particular place of work. In the home office, for example, software and unprepossessing peripheries such as Braille keyboards, Braille printers and speech synthesisers help blind people access the world of the written word. Technical solutions that help resolve communication deficits are in effect aids that provide a virtual means of overcoming the isolation of a home or private apartment. Similarly, the Internet as a global network provides easier access to educa-

tion, enables communication across boundaries, eradicates the monopolies of state-run communication and represents a quantum leap on the road to self-determination. It makes it easier to establish self-help networks and forms the basis for many disabled organisations, without which the current level of coordination at a local, national, and international level would not be possible.

Persistent lobbying for mobility for all

Collaboration between the NGOs has strengthened the disability associations and allowed them to lobby more widely and effectively for their interests. Low-floor wheelchair access to public transport and toilets for the disabled in public spaces and public transport are minimum

....

4   In 1853, the first crash-proof elevator with safety brake was
    introduced in the USA.
5   In 2001, Schindler was awarded the European Union *Breaking
    Barrier Award* for its Miconic 10 lift control system.
6   RFID stands for Radio Frequency Identification.

goals that have nevertheless only come about as a result of dogged lobbying. Significant improvements are not so much the result of general technological advances alone but rather of persistent lobbying which has contributed to their implementation.

Trams

The tramway system in Bern, Switzerland, is a good example of how disabled organisations have successfully brought about improvements:

In 1975, very little attempt was made to cater for the needs of the public. Three unevenly spaced steps had to be negotiated to reach the floor level of the tram 85 cm above ground. Accordingly, only agile passengers were able to use public transport – those who wished to use the tram had to come to terms with the vehicle. Solidly built, these trams are durable and some are still in use today. In 1995, a new model brought significant improvements for the passenger, reducing the floor height to 34 centimetres above ground, accessed via two steps. Nevertheless, the pole between the doors still barred access to wheelchairs! In 2005, the trams now have a single step of 17 centimetres and each door is wide enough to be used by wheelchair users.

Lift and elevator technology

Although the lift has done more to improve the mobility of the disabled than almost any other technological advancement, it has taken almost 150 years since its invention in 1853[4] for elevators to be fully adapted to the specific requirements of the disabled. Elevator sizes large enough for wheelchairs to turn in, control panels mounted lower down, Braille inscriptions and acoustic announcement of floor levels are features that have become industrial standards not so much through technical improvements but as a result of ongoing pressure by disabled organisations.

Further technological improvements have been introduced by the lift manufacturer Schindler with their intelligent destination control system, the Miconic 10.[5] The control system includes functions that cater for the specific needs of the disabled. Lift users choose their destination when calling the lift from a central panel that then indicates which lift will bring them to their destination most quickly. Disabled people can use a special touch-panel. This lets the lift know that the doors should stay open for longer and that the floors should be announced acoustically. Additional access functions are available in combination with a badge-ID or radio-frequency RFID-system.[6]

Electronics assist orientation, safety, and comfort

The combination of miniaturised electronic components, inexpensive processor chips, widespread mobile telecommunications and satellite positioning and navigation systems has sparked new developments that have the potential to provide a hitherto unknown level of support for the mobility needs of disabled people. Some facilities are already undergoing trials in pilot projects:

- Navigation aids based on GPS and RFID technologies allow blind or visually-impaired people to find public services, commercial facilities, and cultural activities on their own, enabling them to take part more actively and independently in public life.
- The combination of medical monitoring equipment, GPS-based positioning devices, and conventional mobile telephones allows people with health restrictions to continue to be mobile in the secure knowledge that medical care can be called immediately.

Such technologies will, however, only prove useful when we are able to establish comprehensive networks based on norms and standards rather than individual solutions – this is the only way to ensure that emerging technological developments serve an inclusive purpose. It is clear that organisations for the disabled will continue to exert the necessary pressure to achieve this.

Sensory technology

Compared with our own extensive sensory faculties and ability to react to stimuli and to communicate, the spectrum of our abilities currently covered by new technology is limited. A reason for this lies in the fact that most people only become aware of their abilities if they lose them to a greater or lesser degree as a result of illness or an accident. The following table provides a simplified[7] overview of our spectrum of perception and potential for communication for each of our sensory organs.

In the same way that the Schindler Award attempts to promote awareness of the experiential world of disabled people in architectural education, so too must such experiences and knowledge inform the interdisciplinary education of mechanical, electronic, and software engineers. The complexity of the "human machine" makes it absolutely necessary to involve biologists, doctors, and psychologists as equal partners in discovering and developing ways in which technology can assist people with disabilities.

....

7   This representation is necessarily simplified: no attempt has been made to represent complex interactions between organs which are responsible, for example, for communications in writing or for emotional responses to information received.

Obstructed perception

What use is technological progress when this is neutralised by our inability to appreciate technological advances? When incompetency hinders the realisation of even the simplest solutions? When reluctance and inhibitions obstruct even the perception of the problem? When educational institutions fail to address the issue of *Access for All* in their curricula? This unhappy situation is not solely attributable to omissions in architectural education; it is a product of a fundamental lack of appreciation, egocentrism and thoughtlessness among us all. The following examples show how a lack of awareness and empathy can lead to technological and emotional discrimination.

The linear markings that provide a tactile means of orientation for the blind are very worn down. We all know the purpose of these lines but as we are not dependent on them ourselves, we pay too little attention to them. In addition, the lines are obstructed by an advertising stand that juts out over them. As the lines mark the most important and direct connections, they also denote the location where intrusive advertising should be placed to be most effective – which was not the original intention…

The holocaust monument is a labyrinth of concrete columns separated by narrow cobble-

Organ	How we perceive our environment	How we communicate
Eyes	Sight	Facial expression, images and writing
Ears	Hearing	
Nose	Smell	Facial expression
Mouth	Taste	Speech, facial expression
Face	Touch (contact, temperature, air movement)	Facial expression
Skin	Touch (contact, temperature, air movement)	Touch
Body hair	Touch (contact, air movement)	Touch
Muscles	Physical resistance, movement, posture	Gesture, mobility
Inner ear	Balance, spatial orientation	

stone passageways. 90% of the passageways are either very narrow, steep or uneven and as a consequence for the majority of the now elderly holocaust survivors no longer navigable. Here it seems we are not even able or willing to realise solutions that can be experienced by a key target group themselves!

On a trip to Vienna to collect photographic material for the Schindler Award, the author of this article noticed a middle-aged man laboriously negotiating a series of steps to an underground station pushing his elderly mother in a wheelchair. The man had obviously overseen the lift and the people rushing past him on the

Bern Railway Station, Switzerland – public transport interchange catering for 10,000 people per day.

stairs or the adjoining escalator seemed unaware of the situation. The author volunteered his help and took hold of the wheelchair. A surprising situation ensued: although until then no-one had apparently noticed his predicament, many people suddenly offered their assistance and the wheelchair was too small for everyone to hold onto. It seems that the fear of making contact is a barrier that is also difficult to overcome.

This example from recent political discourse in Switzerland illustrates just how problematic and inhibited our perception of disabilities still is. While the referendum on changes in the law did not shake the fundamental basis of disability insurance, the reforms would result in significant reductions in insurance provisions in certain areas. The unions embarked on a postcard campaign to protest against the reforms showing photomontages of the responsible politicians as potential victims. The justice minister was depicted with an amputated leg, the finance minister as an alcoholic, and the health minister in a wheelchair. While the majority of disabled people welcomed the campaign, many "normal" people found the approach "vulgar," "degrading," "indescribable" or even "denigrating." It is, however, not so much a lack of respect that troubles people, as a basic reflex to suppress and screen out disabled people and their disabilities. What we do not see, we do not have to deal with – if it doesn't affect us, we don't need to take any action.

Normalisation

Disabilities are relative. Different individual abilities are normalised according to a variety of categories and average levels of ability are declared a norm, an official designation of what is "normal" – anything that deviates from the norm may then be stigmatised as a disability or special case. By establishing norms we are discriminating. It is our adherence to norms that actu-

Berlin, Holocaust Monument by Richard Serra and Peter Eisenman.

Postcard campaign accompanying the Swiss referendum. The justice minister depicted with an amputated leg (photomontage).

ally makes anything not conforming to the norm a disability. The more tolerant society is, the more able we are to accept variance, and the wider is our notion of what constitutes normal-

ity. The more tolerant society is, the more people are able to make full use of their abilities for the good of all, and to contribute to the development of society without fear of stigmatisation.

Public utility –
Car sharing as a complementary means of urban mobility
Willi Loose

Car sharing as a means of extending mobility

Mobility is generally described by transport economists as the ability or willingness to move from one place to another. Accordingly, accessible mobility means the provision of different modes of transport that are easier for people with restricted mobility or mobility handicaps to use with a view to enabling *Access for All*. To this end, often elaborate building measures are undertaken to remove existing barriers such as stairs, steps and changes in level or to insert lifts into multi-storey buildings.

Car sharing extends the palette of available modes of transport by offering a personal means of mobility that is well suited to urban environments and, at the same time, contributes to reducing the dominance of cars in our cities. As an organised and communal form of vehicular transport it complements existing modes of environmentally-friendly public transport, such as bus and train, bicycle or walking. The only prerequisite for being able to use this service is a valid driving license and the need to sign up with a professional car sharing provider or become a member of a car sharing association, many of which are run by volunteers.

From grassroots initiative to professional mobility service in 20 years

The first car sharing initiative in Germany was founded in 1988 in Berlin, one year after the es-

Fifty new low-emission vehicles for "cambio Bremen."

tablishment of a car sharing scheme in Switzerland. Since then, the idea has spread rapidly throughout the larger cities in Germany resulting in a network of decentralised associations. Today there are around 110 independent providers on the market, and in larger conurbations, these have even begun to compete with one another. The idea of organised car sharing was born out of the ecology movement and has developed continually since then without state aid or outside investors in the form of countless self-help initiatives.

Today, thanks to the pioneering work of the first generation, the branch is now so well established that it has attracted the interest of larger, wealthier companies from other economic sectors, as the recent market offerings by some of the larger car rental companies or the Daimler Group have shown. This is a significant achievement given the fact that the ownership of a car, or more than one car, is generally regarded as a status symbol, or at the very least as synonymous with being equally able to participate in public life. It is a model that continues to receive strong political backing despite negative side effects for energy consumption and the climate.

Nevertheless, the idea of car sharing has become more and more socially acceptable and is even being openly discussed at a strategic management level by well-known car manufac-

turers. In an anniversary publication commemorating 100 years of the DVWG German Association of Transport Sciences, Eckhard Minx, director of the DaimlerChrysler Society and Technology Research Group, elaborated a vision in which car manufacturers may in future sell less cars and instead offer customers guaranteed long-term use of their chosen model via a service contract agreement.[1] And indeed, in autumn 2008, the Daimler Group initiated the "Car2go" programme, a pilot project that resembles car sharing. Initially, the trial period was restricted to Daimler staff and their families in and around the city of Ulm, Germany, but as of spring 2009, the pilot programme has gone public with 200 "Smart" cars in the Ulm region.

At the beginning of 2009, over 137,000 car sharing users were registered with providers in Germany. This represents a 20% rise in 2008 due to the fact that car sharing was able to profit from generally unfavourable conditions for car owners, such as the high cost of petrol, expensive car prices and the lack of parking spaces in inner cities. The undisputed champion of car sharing is, however, Switzerland which has almost seven times as many car sharing users in proportion to the population.

Car sharing is currently available in around 270 cities and municipalities in Germany. Over the last year, commercial car sharing providers and associations have again endeavoured to po-

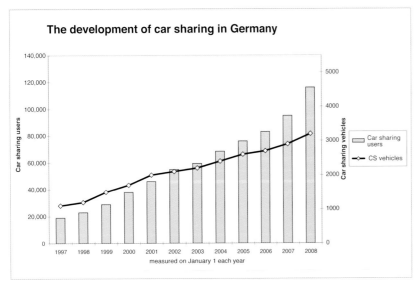

The development of car sharing in Germany from 1997 to 2009.

1   Eckhard Minx, Thomas Waschke, "Mobilität von morgen –
    Konzepte der Automobilindustrie," in: Deutsche Verkehrswis-
    senschaftliche Gemeinschaft (ed.): *100 Jahre DVWG*. Berlin
    2008.

"Greenwheels" car sharing stations in Amsterdam, Netherlands.

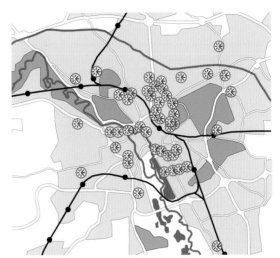

"Stadtmobil Hannover" car sharing stations in Hanover, Germany.

sition their services closer to where private or commercial users live and work, establishing decentralised pick-up points or stations dispersed throughout the city. As a result, a car for communal use situated just around the corner with its own dedicated parking space has become reality in many more built-up urban areas. Traditional car owners, on the other hand, must circle repeatedly in order to find a parking space nearby. The figure on the right shows the spatial distribution of car sharing stations in the city of Hanover, which corresponds to that of many other larger cities. Here one can see that there are comparatively few users in neighbourhoods with a high proportion of social housing or in outlying districts that consist predominantly of villas. In these areas, the number of car sharing stations is correspondingly smaller.

Car sharing in Germany has also becoming increasingly popular among business users. Shared vehicles offer an alternative means of mobility for many companies, offices, agencies and organisations which staff can make use of when own company car facilities are stretched, or as a cheaper alternative to using own vehicles for business journeys. Almost 23% of car sharing users are company employees who use car sharing services regularly or sporadically for business-related trips. For the providers, a mixture of private and business customers is advantageous as these users' respective periods of demand complement one another, ensuring a relatively even level of vehicle usage. Business customers use car sharing services primarily during the day on weekdays while private use peaks in the evenings and at the weekend.

The elements of a modern car sharing system

All larger providers employ modern, customer-friendly technological systems that have been custom-developed for car sharing services and are now also being adopted for commercial fleet management. For example, for the FIFA World Cup in Germany in 2006, the entire VIP-fleet was managed using a technological system that originated from the car sharing sector. Investment by the providers made it possible to develop it further to its current operational state. A customer-centred car sharing concept is characterised by the following qualities:

■ A fleet of modern vehicles including a series of different models to cover all typical user requirements. In accordance with demand, around 70% of the vehicles are compact car models. These cover most general day-to-day requirements in the city and surrounding areas. Estate cars, minibuses and small vans are provided to cater for shopping trips or family trips at the weekend.

■ Dedicated stations or pick-up and drop points exclusively for car sharing vehicles are located as close as possible to where private users live or in business districts where they can serve multiple business customers. These are typically densely-populated, mixed-use inner city neighbourhoods. The aim is to ensure that car sharing vehicles are always close at hand so that their use can be easily integrated into people's everyday way of life. The distribution of the stations generally follows the pattern of customer growth. Unfortunately, in many towns, providers are not always able to find appropriate parking spaces in densely-built, inner-city neighbourhoods, whether on private land or in publicly accessible car parks.

■ For the future development of the branch, it will be necessary to establish a nationwide statutory regulation that allows the creation of car sharing stations on public streets. This is a matter of increasing urgency. Some cities have already taken a step in this direction by implementing special arrangements of their own. In Weimar, for example, a car sharing station has been established on the Goetheplatz in the city centre.

....

2 ADAC e.V., Verkehrspolitik und Verbraucherschutz (ed.):
   Kfz-Anschaffung und -Unterhaltung 2007. Munich 2008.

- It is possible to make vehicle bookings around the clock, either online or by telephone. In some cases, bookings can be made as text messages sent from a mobile phone. Bookings can be made several days in advance or at short notice – provided the desired vehicle is not already booked. For example, a user submitting a booking via mobile telephone may be able to use a vehicle within around two minutes – as soon as the booking system transmits a confirmation of reservation by text message to the on-board computer in the car.
- The larger providers employ electronic access control systems in conjunction with a chip card issued to the customer along with instructions when they register. With a so-called stand-alone system, access to the car is gained via a combination of remote activation of the on-board computer and a card ID reader mounted behind the windscreen. Alternatively, a key deposit box located near to the car is sometimes used where several vehicles are available from the same location.

Car sharing station on the Goetheplatz in Weimar.

Flexible costs due to low fixed cost ratio

The increasing attraction of car sharing is a logical consequence of proven cost efficiency. According to the German Automobile Association ADAC, the cost index for running a privately owned car had risen by 20% by the end of 2007 compared with the year 2000 while in the same period, disposable income had stagnated or even decreased.[2] Private car ownership has therefore become a disproportionately large cost factor. According to fuel cost prognoses, this looks unlikely to change in the future.

Fixed costs constitute a large proportion of the cost of private car ownership, most notably value depreciation which typically amounts to several hundred Euros per month. As a result, new car owners use their car for many journeys that they previously undertook using other means of transport: "The car cost us so much, so we should now use it properly" is a common

Stand-alone car unlocking system using an electronic chip card and sensor mounted behind the windscreen.

"Car2go" Ulm user instructions via on-board computer.

mentality among new car owners. With car sharing the fixed costs are spread across many shoulders. This explains its cost advantage, which on average applies up to an annual usage of around 10,000 kilometres, provided one doesn't need a car on a daily basis. In addition, the cost component of each and every journey is listed with each billing. This motivates users to consider whether all journeys really need to be undertaken with a car or whether perhaps another form of public transport, bicycling or walking might be more appropriate. Car sharing makes the concealed costs of mobility visible so that consumers can factor these costs into eve-

ryday personal expenditure. It also keeps open the option of using multiple modes of transport, unlike private car ownership which tends to displace the use of other means of transport.

Car sharing reduces emissions and impact on the urban environment

The following summarises a series of findings from recent scientific studies on the impact of car sharing on the environment and traffic load. The beneficial effects of car sharing are based on separate individual effects which in combination reinforce one another:

....

3   The study encompassed 1042 car sharing vehicles available for hire through the DB-Carsharing tarif.

4   Andreas Knie, Weert Canzler, *Die intermodalen Dienste der Bahn: Wirkungen und Potenziale neuer Verkehrsdienstleistungen*. Joint final report by DB Rent and the WZB on

the transport network project "Intermodi – Sicherung der Anschluss- und Zugangsmobilität durch neue Angebotsbausteine im Rahmen der 'Forschungsinitiative Schiene'", Förderkennzeichen 19 P 2049 A + B. Berlin 2005, p. 51.

Car sharing vehicles have a lower fuel consumption than most average private cars and produce lower levels of emissions.

In Germany, car sharing vehicles are on average newer than the average age of private cars. With the exception of smaller associations, most providers renew their car pools every three to four years. Technological improvements to vehicles that help reduce their impact on the environment are put into effect at a faster rate than with private vehicles.

According to a study by the WZB Social Science Research Centre in Berlin,[3] car fleets managed by the larger urban car sharing providers exhibit on average 16% less specific carbon dioxide emissions compared with the national average for new private vehicles.[4] A contributing factor is that the majority of car sharing vehicles have less horse power than the average private car and that different vehicles can be chosen according to the kind of journey.

Each car sharing vehicle replaces on average between four to eight private vehicles!

Many private car sharing users and some business users sell their own car once they

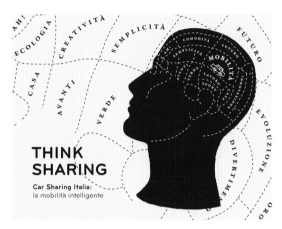

Advertising for car sharing in Italy.

join a car sharing arrangement, or at least shelve plans to purchase a new car.

Car sharing reduces pressure on parking spaces in inner city neighbourhoods, also making it easier for private car owners to park.

The reduction in car ownership as a result of an increased uptake in car sharing leads – in terms of figures – to a reduction in the space required for vehicles. These areas can be then used for other purposes more beneficial for the city. For example, parking spaces can be

....

5 Around half of all households in those areas where a choice was possible have officially declared their households to be car-free, obviating their need to create a parking space. A large proportion of these households participate in the local car sharing scheme. Twelve car sharing vehicles have been provided for their use.

converted into more space for bicycle paths or pedestrians. The redesign of urban street-space and the creation of public spaces can also contribute to improving the quality of life in urban areas. For example, in the newly built Vauban quarter in the city of Freiburg, parking spaces set aside for households that are officially designated as car-free are "given back" to the local residents in the form of green, recreational areas.[5]

■ Car sharing as a means of tackling climate change.

In 2006, a study undertaken to examine the impact of car sharing in Switzerland came to the conclusion that car sharing users in Switzerland produce 290 kg less carbon dioxide emissions per year than they would if car sharing was not available (theoretical control situation).[6] This value is a factor of the afore-mentioned lower level of specific fuel consumption for car journeys as well as the overall use of more ecologically-friendly modes of transport for the sum of all journeys undertaken. As a result, car sharing is an effective means of tackling climate change that many

Parking spaces set aside for car-free households in the Vauban Quarter of Freiburg. If the households were to purchase cars, parking spaces would have to be provided here.

people can contribute to individually. In political terms, promoting car sharing is a cost-effective means of tackling the greenhouse effect and, in addition, is viewed positively.

Car sharing – a form of motorised mobility ideally suited to compact cities

In the above we have seen that car sharing not only extends the available means of personal

6   Ueli Haefeli, Daniel Matti, Christoph Schreyer, Markus Maibach, *Evaluation Car-Sharing*. Final report commissioned by the BFE / SFOE Swiss Federal Office for Energy, Bern 2006.

mobility and augments other modes of public transport but also alleviates the effects of traffic on the city and the environment. The fact that such services are comparatively ecologically-friendly and can contribute to urban development means that overall they contribute to the common good. At the same time, they also benefit others who do not themselves use the service, such as those who continue to use their own car. Every additional car sharing vehicle makes the concept more appealing and attracts new customers. This is confirmed by the high level of customer satisfaction that has been voiced in numerous surveys in different cities. Satisfied customers and word-of-mouth recommendations to friends, colleagues and family are the best form of advertising for the branch. Car sharing represents a form of motorised mobility ideally suited to the denser urban environments of compact cities. It has taken several decades to slow the pattern of migration away from the cities to the regions and the accompanying unrestrained settlement of green field sites, which in turn has led to increasing levels of car ownership. Today, a countermovement is emerging where sections of the population are beginning to return to the inner cities of urban conurbations. In the compact inner cities, however, there is not enough space to continue the same pattern of car usage as practiced in the suburbs. Car sharing offers a suitable alternative – to a private car or a second car – by providing people with motorised transport as and when they need it. And, unlike with private car ownership, the potential and possibility to use other forms of public transport where appropriate remains an attractive and also realistic choice. In short, car sharing offers as much motorised transport as required with as little impact as possible!

. . . .

For further information see:
www.carsharing.de

Reflection –
Philosophy for everyone?
Gernot Böhme

1. Barriers to access

The respect accorded to philosophy in public is generally accompanied by a peculiar shyness, a sense of unease, of head-shaking perplexity, and stalwart proponents of *common sense* may at times even treat it with contempt: philosophy, so it seems, is incomprehensible, extreme, arrogant, out of touch, in short abstruse. This ambivalent reception of philosophy is almost certainly grounded in its claim to be applicable for each and every one of us while simultaneously denying that people in their everyday behaviour fully realise the qualities by which human existence is defined. However, long before such ambivalent claims can come into effect, there are barriers to be overcome that hinder, or even obstruct, the average person's ability to engage in philosophy. And these have less to do with the actual nature of philosophy than with its fate as an academic discipline.

Philosophy can be regarded as the mother of all sciences. It is, after all, Socratic inquiry into the nature of things and its tireless insistence on substantiating knowledge that first brought about the desire to anchor knowledge *qua science*. At this time, philosophy was not actually a science in itself but rather a means of approaching science and a discipline that presided over methodology. Even after the founding of the first universities in Europe, the role of philosophy remained unchanged for hundreds of years: the philosophy faculty served as a preparatory propaedeutic through which every student had to pass before entering one of the actual professional faculties: theology, medicine, and jurisprudence. This relationship between philosophy and science first began to change with the emergence of the modern university from around the 18th century onwards. Although philosophy remained a propaedeuticum for many scientific disciplines until well into the 20th century, it also had to adapt to the spirit of the universities and that meant that philosophy could only defend its position as an academic discipline by developing into a science in its own right. A lengthy process of transition began, shaped for example by Kant's endeavours to establish a critical philosophy and explicitly elucidated by Husserl in 1900 in his paper *Philosophy as a Rigorous Science*. In contemporary university studies, philosophy is no longer a preparatory or supplementary discipline but stands alongside other sciences as a science of its own kind. That means it has its own curricula, its own methods and own qualifications. It also means it has its own problems. The work of a professional philosopher today is primarily concerned with problems raised by the discipline itself. It relates to a particular state of re-

Immanuel Kant.

....

1   Gernot Böhme, *Einführung in die Philosophie.*
    Weltweisheit – Lebensform – Wissenschaft, Suhrkamp,
    4th edition, Frankfurt a. M. 2001.

search or discourse and in turn refers for the most part to work undertaken previously by other colleagues. It seeks responses and recognition from others in the field, that is, from the academic discipline of philosophy.

This seems to me a very restricted understanding of philosophy. In my *Introduction to Philosophy*[1] I differentiate between three kinds of philosophising: philosophy as a way of life or mode of living, philosophy as practical wisdom and philosophy as a science. One can immediately see that according to this division, what is officially regarded as philosophy, namely the academic discipline, constitutes only one third of what belongs to philosophy – those aspects that one can describe as a science. Philosophy as a mode of living describes a way of philosophising on an everyday basis that recalls Socrates' vision of a philosophical way of life. Philosophy as a "practical wisdom" (*Weltweisheit*) describes – according to Immanuel Kant, who at that time already endeavoured to distinguish this from the so-called philosophy of the schools – the kind of philosophy that is concerned with "what interests everyone," that is with questions of public importance. As such, this kind of philosophising is not concerned with issues brought forward by professional colleagues but with the broader problems facing society at large.

Our awareness of philosophy as more than what is dealt with in the academic realm has never entirely vanished. Characteristic of this is Wolfgang Wieland's remark that one should differentiate between philosophers and professors of philosophy. Admittedly, the term *philosopher* can be understood nowadays as an occupational title and therefore academic professors of philosophy are indeed also philosophers. Wieland's remark, however, implies that to hold the status of a philosopher, one needs much more than simply academic knowledge of the discipline of philosophy.

Among the barriers that make it difficult for many people to engage in philosophy, we can identify three in particular: its language, its abstract nature of thought and to a certain extent the radical nature of philosophy itself.

Here the term *language* points in turn to barriers erected by the aforementioned scholarly "scientisation" and professionalisation of philosophy. Every academic discipline develops its own language and terminology, and without appropriate social awareness of this terminology, one is unable to fully understand the knowledge of the respective discipline. In the case of philosophy there is a further aspect that differentiates it from other disciplines: its historicity. Specific academic terminologies generally have an instrumental character and their meaning depends only on the current definition. This is not the case with philosophy. Philosophical terminology almost always has a historical dimension. For this reason, it would be illusory to believe that one need only adhere to the current usage as each term is always accompanied by a diffuse cluster of historical connotations. This applies in particular to terms such as *substance*, *quality*, *identity*, and *causality*. By way of example, I will briefly consider a less ambiguous term: *quintessence*. This expression is rooted in Plato's attempt to link the concept of the four elements with his at-the-time new and most impressive concept of the five platonic solids. These five solids describe perfectly symmetrical convex bodies in three-dimensional space: the tetrahedron, cube, octahedron, dodecahedron and the icosahedron. When relating these solids to the four elements, fire, water, earth and air, Plato had one solid left over which he attributed, partly out of a need to resolve the predicament and partly as ironic gesture, to the universe as a whole. Plato's pupil Philip of Opus, who is credited with completing Plato's unfinished *Epinomis*, attempted to resolve the predicament through systematic consideration, reasoning that five platonic bodies necessitated five distinct elements. Accordingly he attributed the fifth body to the ether. As a consequence, the ether became the quintessence, the fifth essence. Since then, fuelled in particular by the practice of alchemy, all manner of interpretations of the quintessence have been developed, including among, others, Paracelsus' assertion that man himself could be the quintessence. To truly understand the language of philosophy, one needs to be aware of such historical connotations.

A second barrier to engaging in philosophy is the abstractness of philosophical thought. Abstractness is not the same as generality – the latter is shared by all sciences not just philosophy. The abstractness of philosophical thought refers to the fact that the issues under consideration are rarely tangible or perceptible. Rather they are gained through reflection or through speculation. Characteristic of this approach is the process of nominalisation, which in the Greek or German languages is achieved very easily through the addition of a preceding article. A word used as a verb in everyday language such as *sein* (to be) is converted into a noun, *das Sein* (being) – and immediately we have the subject of an entire philosophical discipline, namely ontology. For the layman this process is, shall we say, somewhat confusing; it is as if suddenly one is left with nothing to stand on. One no longer knows, at least not immediately, what is being talked about. The topic has shifted to things that one cannot experience directly but nevertheless ultimately form the basis of how

....

2   *Kritik der reinen Vernunft* A158/B197; Immanuel Kant, *Critique of Pure Reason*, Transl. by Norman Kemp Smith, St. Martin's Press, New York 1965, p. 194.

one experiences things at all. The philosopher Immanuel Kant described this type of thinking as *transcendental*. In his *Critique of Pure Reason* he strives to elaborate the conditions of all possible experience. He offers an answer in his first principle, according to which "the conditions of the possibility of experience in general are likewise conditions of the possibility of the objects of experience."[2] Here we have a prime example of a philosophical sentence which is extremely difficult to decipher. It requires that we do what Plato has described as "turning our whole soul inside out" by averting our gaze from empirically experienced objects and directing our attention to that which is purely thought – with the concomitant promise that only then will we be able to properly understand that which we experience empirically. Philosophy therefore demands of all those willing to engage in it that, at the very moment of engaging, they adopt a way of thinking contrary to *common sense*. Truth is not to be found through direct confrontation but rather through indirect, reflexive consideration. What is given to us is explained through what is not given to us; the concrete is explained by the abstract.

This tendency towards abstraction can also be attributed to the third aforementioned barrier, that of the radical nature of philosophical thought. The word *radical* is related to *radix*, to roots, and indeed philosophy is radical in as far as it is concerned with fundamentals, with principles, with origins and beginnings. Consequently, philosophy is also *paradoxical* in the literal sense; it goes against what we commonly believe, against preconceptions. Those who are interested in philosophy are expected to put aside everything they have believed until now and to call into question the balance and securities that have been the basis of their sense of certainty in everyday life. Our day-to-day thinking is, generally speaking, governed by compromises that mediate between conflicting tendencies and opinions. For the most part, our thinking balances one thing with another. Compared with this, philosophical thought is radical and requires that at first we pursue a train of thought to its conclusion, without regard to other considerations or counter-arguments.

In an age in which people increasingly seek to establish resonance for their ideas through media publicity and in which the reputation of philosophers is likewise made through the media, philosophy's fundamental trait towards radicalness translates into scandal: that which is radical and contradicts common sense can through the media assume scandalous proportions. One example from the comparatively recent past is Peter Sloterdijk's speech *Regulations for the Human Park* and his talk of anthropotechnics therein. A more recent example is Giorgio Agamben's book *Homo sacer* in which he mythologises the victims of the concentration camps, stripped down to their bare life, by subsuming them under a term used in ancient Roman law: *homo sacer*. The radicalness of his train of thought culminates in the sentence: "today it is not the *polis* but rather the camp that is the fundamental biopolitical paradigm of the West."[3]

In using such a sentence Agamben profits from the morbid fascination that continues to surround the crimes of the Nazis to the present day. The radical nature of his approach manifests itself in the assertion that the administration of human life – when thought through to its conclusion – tends towards its very destruction, whereas the reproduction of human life happens on its own. Real biopolitics is, of course, always primarily – or ostensibly, as Agamben argues – directed towards the reproduction of life.

2. Philosophy as practical wisdom

The accessibility of philosophy is by definition very different when used as "practical wisdom." Here philosophy is actively oriented towards the general public as it is concerned with what interests and involves everyone, and because it aims to be effective in the public arena. Philosophy as practical wisdom consists predominantly of criticism. The reason for this lies in the fact that philosophy can and must participate in the resolution of matters of public interest through its own means and methods. For the most part, the problems facing society require political, juridical and economic solutions. However, there is one aspect where philosophy is well-nigh indispensable in the resolution of public questions: the question of how these problems are thought about in the first place. It is not uncommon to find that public issues are dealt with in public in a way that does not solve the problem but in a sense actually prolongs it. This is the case whenever the way of thinking is itself part of the problem. An example helps here to illustrate what I mean. Approaches to dealing with environmental issues generally revolve around a notion of nature, in which nature is defined as that which occurs naturally – and as such is deemed good. Consequently, a key strategy is to conserve the natural environment: the supposition is that one can address environmental problems by protecting what is endangered by human intervention. In actual fact what one wishes to preserve is not natural in the true

....

3   Giorgio Agamben, *Homo sacer. Sovereign Power and Bare Life.* Stanford University Press, Chicago 1998, p. 181.

Sokrates.

sense of the word but in most cases already a historical product of human interaction with nature. The actual natural environments in question are themselves rarely defined purely in natural terms but instead socially, for example in terms of land ownership and land use interests. Philosophy can help demonstrate that employing a classical notion of nature to deal with environmental problems is dysfunctional. If nature is that which needs to be protected against human intervention, it will over time be pushed back ever further. Instead nature needs in these cases to be conceived of as something that has already been shaped by human involvement.[4]

Another problem where the way it has been approached obstructs its solution is the inadequate psychosocial support of pregnant and childbearing women. Here one can easily show that the traditional knowledge of midwives encompasses practices that fulfil the human needs of expectant mothers. A closer inspection of modern-day obstetrics, as practised by gynaecologists, reveals that it is unable to fulfil the psychosocial needs of mothers-to-be due to its objectified and technological approach. Given this, the correct response would be to revive and strengthen the empirical knowledge of midwives. Instead, the primacy of scientific knowledge is such that midwives have long become

socially subordinate to doctors, so that under the prevailing conditions a strengthening of the role of midwives would mean the professionalisation of midwifery through the introduction of scientific training. Here too a particular way of thinking – in this case the assumption that scientific knowledge is the best form of knowledge – has characterised the problem so deeply that it cannot be resolved and will in fact be perpetuated through the proposed solution. In this case a philosophical criticism of forms of knowledge would have helped to break down the structure of preconceptions and in turn contribute to the resolution of this issue of public importance.[5]

3. Philosophy as a mode of living

Although philosophy as a mode of living or way of life is no longer part of scientific philosophy, this does not mean that it has been entirely forgotten at a broader level. On the contrary, the philosophy of the Stoa – that is from a time in which philosophy was a practical part of everyday life for large sections of the population – still has a loyal following. Authors such as Epictetus, Seneca, and Marc Aurel are still among the bestselling classical philosophers. Their writings offer consolation and guidance for greater peace of mind and level-headedness

....

4   Gernot Böhme, Engelbert Schramm (ed.), *Soziale Naturwissenschaft. Wege zur Erweiterung der Ökologie*, Fischer, Frankfurt a. M. 1985.

5   Gernot Böhme, "Midwifery as Science: An Essay on the Relation between Scientific and Everyday Knowledge", in:

N. Stehr, V. Meja (eds.), *Society and Knowledge. Contemporary Perspectives in the Sociology of Knowledge*, Transaction Books, New Brunswick/London 1984, pp. 365–385.

and champion the ideal of wisdom. Whether, however, the classical ideal of a philosophical mode of life, that of self-control, self-sufficiency, autonomy and ataraxy can still be a model for leading a philosophical life in the present day is perhaps questionable. Until such questions have been debated in full, it could be that the classical notion of a philosophical mode of living serves more of a compensatory role, and therefore a masking function, in the context of modern day life.

How exactly philosophy as a mode of living should be defined is something that, in my view, must be examined anew in every age – it has to be able to respond to the contemporary living conditions; it has to defend humanity against the deformatory or levelling tendencies of the day. If we can describe our modern day living conditions as that of technological civilisation, we can see that under these conditions the modern way of living is in many respects a trivialised fulfilment of the classical ideal of a philosophical conduct of life. Where the ideal of classical philosophy promotes a way of living not subject to the vagaries and upheavals of emotion and circumstance, we can note today that most people's lives are on average relatively uneventful and unemotional and that institutionalised safety mechanisms exist that reduce

the risk of biographical catastrophes. Where self-control was central to the classical ideal of a philosophical conduct of life, today we can say that everyone more or less fulfils this ideal in a trivial manner, for example when driving a car. Most people can behave calmly and soberly independent of their respective emotional situation – although not actually through self-control but rather through the compartmentalisation of behavioural responses. If we continue in this way to address each of the individual aspects of the classical philosophical mode of living, we see that they are indeed fulfilled in modern life, though not emphatically; rather, in a trivialised form. A new question arises as a consequence of this analysis: in what way do our average living conditions, particularly the technically regulated living conditions, influence our ability to experience ourselves and our lives as human beings? I would like to elaborate on just two examples. The first concerns our physical bodily experience, our sense of suffering and our pathic existence in general. The second concerns our own existence in the sense of our consciousness of being in the present.

In our civilisation, people have long been driven by an active conception of the self and in today's work and achievement-oriented society, this self-conception is largely defined through

Plato.

one's activities and achievements. This has, among other things, resulted in an understanding of ethics almost solely in terms of an ethics of actions. All those human aspects where we are given to ourselves, where things happen to us, where we suffer, are by contrast neglected. We are not equipped with the appropriate competencies to deal with these and such phenomena are either masked or simply unknown; those moments where we are left to ourselves do not contribute to our own sense of identity. This applies particularly to our own bodies, that part of nature which we experience as ourselves, despite the fact that, or perhaps precisely because, we do not produce it ourselves. Innately linked with this is the feeling of pain, or more generally of suffering, which we understand as something to be overcome, something to be cast out of the self. Despite this, we are able to comprehend that the self, of which we modern day citizens are so proud, is on the face of it empty without things that directly impinge on us. We are consequently far from an understanding of ourselves as affected beings. This is precisely where philosophy as a mode of living can apply today. It would be concerned with regaining a sense of bodily experience, a positive comprehension of suffering, the development of virtues of pathic existence or, in more modern terms, the development of competencies that allow us to actually experience things that happen to us.

A philosophical development of such competencies could also have very practical consequences. It would, for example, be a prerequisite for being able to fulfil the needs of self-assured patients. Over and above the medicinal appraisal of the advantages and disadvantages of particular therapies, the patients would themselves be able to contribute through a readiness to "embed" a particular therapy in their conception of themselves and their desired way of life. Such decisions can only be made when the patient really feels at home in his body, that is to say that his body is truly his own and he knows how to integrate illness and suffering in his conception of himself.

The second example that I mentioned of a way in which a philosophical mode of living in the present day could counteract a loss of humanity concerns the terms *existence* and the *consciousness of being in the present*. One can argue that both classical philosophy's attempts to cultivate a sense of self as well as Christianity's strivings for spiritual salvation aim to overcome the weakness and vulnerability of human existence in the immediacy of the moment or – as Christianity calls it – to dominate the animality of human existence. This is, of course, grounded in the fact that such direct and immediate existence, with its charms and challenges and also its volatile, transitory character, was experienced as a burden and also with a sense of continual loss. In contrast to this, one erected the ideals of a purely spiritual existence, of eternal life and salvation in the hereafter. Today one can contend that human existence is no longer directly experienced at all and is in a sense devoid of the present. The modern day consciousness of man has been divided on the one hand into projections and intentions, i.e. imagined notions of the future, and on the other into memories and justification strategies, i.e. an awareness of the past. We compensate for our inability to exist in the present through documentation, for example through recorded sound and images which chronicle what we should have experienced directly so that we may take them in as fact after the event. This lack of consciousness of the present also translates as a disregard for actual physical presence and the inability to experience sensations aesthetically. What we are missing out on is in actual fact life itself, the very vitality of being, in as far as we are able to fully experience it. As a consequence, modern day man is missing out on the most elementary form of happiness, namely the happiness of being.[6] Instead he seeks happiness in riches, in the good things in life. He spends his lifetime acquiring these and is then all too often unable to enjoy them fully.

Against this background, a philosophical mode of living should be concerned with recovering the direct experience of being. It should consist of practices that school attentiveness and perception and would seek the suspension or, as one would say in philosophy, the bracketing out – the *epoche* – of all intentions as well as argumentation, in short of all forms of justificatory discourse. This modern day approach would, in stark contrast therefore to the classical ideal of a philosophical mode of living, be concerned with the directness of experience, with the ability to immerse oneself in the present and with the development of a consciousness of how we live our lives. This will be almost impossible to achieve without the help of meditative practices. Except that in this case, in contrast to the classical philosophical ideal, these would not be of the kind in which one aspires to eternal truths but the very opposite, those in which one can submerge oneself in the present in all its sensory richness and in one's own existence as we experience it in all its physical vitality.

In the same way that philosophy as a practical wisdom is open to everyone in as far as it is concerned with problems that interest everyone, so too philosophy as a mode of living is not subject to professional barriers. Of course, the

....

6 Gernot Böhme, "Das Glück, da zu sein," in: R. J. Kozljanič (ed.), *II. Jahrbuch für Lebensphilosophie*, Albunea Verlag, Munich 2006, pp. 209–218. Also in: Renate Breuninger (ed.), *Glück*, Humboldt-Studienzentrum, Ulm 2006, pp. 57–69.

same applies today as ever: philosophy as a practical wisdom entails in essence a shift in thinking and the overcoming of preconceptions while philosophy as a mode of living consists primarily in a reversal and a revision of the prevailing behavioural patterns set down by technical civilisation and an efficiency-driven society.

To cite Kant, one could also say that to lead a philosophical life today means to assume responsibility for one's life, to neither allow one's life to simply pass – that is to consign oneself to the respective trends and fashions – nor to allow experts to dictate the way one lives one's life.

Internet –
Digital inclusion for everyone regardless of their abilities
Jutta Croll

Internet for all – digital inclusion

The term digital divide was coined in the mid-1990s in the USA by the National Telecommunications and Information Administration (NTIA)[1] in its *Falling through the Net* report, which identified a divide between those groups of society who have access to information and communication technologies and those who have not. In Germany too there are debates on the different possibilities various societal groups have when it comes to accessing digital media and the Internet in particular. The overall aim of ensuring equal access to and use of new media for all sections of society is described as *digital inclusion*, or, at a European level, also as *e-inclusion*.

In recent years a more differentiated view of how to realise this aim has arisen that focuses not solely on providing general access to the Internet but also takes into account the heterogeneity of the respective disadvantaged societal groups and recognises that individual approaches are necessary that are appropriate to particular sub-groups and their respective specific living conditions. In addition to providing access to the Internet, such measures must therefore also help users to make appropriate use of what digital media have to offer. For those groups of society that are disadvantaged with respect to Internet usage – the elderly, immigrants, socially or educationally disadvantaged people as well

as parts of the rural population – these measures include providing specific targeted programmes for communicating media skills as well as facilitating opportunities where digital media can be experienced first-hand. The digital inclusion of people with disabilities is achieved primarily through the increased number of websites that are designed in such a way that they can also be used by these target groups.

Barriers in the Internet

People with disabilities are confronted by a variety of different kinds of barriers when using the Internet. Internet users without physical or mental disabilities often find it difficult to comprehend that this medium can also be used by people with disabilities when designed appropriately. The barriers that obstruct usage of the Internet often only become apparent once one becomes aware how Internet content is perceived and how particular functions of websites are used or once the handicapped users' specific culture of communication is understood.

Blind people are able to use the Internet with the help of a so-called *screen reader* or a refreshable Braille display. A screen reader is a software programme installed on the user's computer that reads out loud what appears on the screen – at least what is present as text or has been annotated as text in the source code.

Parallel usage of a Braille display and keyboard.

By hearing what is read out aloud, blind people are able to access the same content other people see. A refreshable Braille display translates the same content into Braille characters, presenting them using a system of protruding and retractable studs that can be felt. Blind or partially sighted people are reliant on being able to use the keyboard to navigate websites as they are unable to perceive the position of the cursor or mouse pointer. The user can switch from one link to the next by pressing the tab key; pressing the return-key visits the link.

For people with impaired motor functions, the usability of navigation and functional elements in a website – for example input boxes in forms – might be a problem. Special input devices that replace the mouse, or speech recog-

nition software for controlling the computer through spoken commands, can assist these users in using the Internet.

Deaf or hearing-impaired users are unable to access any information that is available exclusively in acoustic form. In addition, deaf people very often lack written language skills as for many, particularly those who are deaf from birth, sign language is their mother tongue; they have to learn the written almost like a foreign language. Complicated syntax and the use of technical jargon, professional language, or foreign words represent a barrier to understanding. Sign language videos can be used to present complex issues in a form appropriate for deaf people. They understand the text by seeing the hand and mouth movements of the person on the screen. People with learning difficulties or reading or spelling difficulties such as dyslexia can also find it difficult to understand content in text form. Further barriers include the inconsistent use of symbols and terminology and complex navigational structures and interaction methods.

Accessible websites – straightforward for everyone

For people with disabilities, the ability to use the Internet offers clear advantages: the Internet helps them overcome limitations in their ability

1 www.ntia.doc.gov

to lead their lives independently such as mobility restrictions or limited ability or opportunity to communicate. Digital media can offer them an equal opportunity to take part in society. A precondition for this is the accessible design of websites and their contents, and an awareness of the respective target group's specific usage requirements when accessing online services. It is not just disabled users who benefit from such design considerations. Accessible websites generally require less bandwidth so that they load more quickly and can also be used on mobile devices with small displays. Clear and communicative navigation structures – which accessible websites should offer – also help fledgling users with less experience of using web-based services. The use of plain language helps people with migrant backgrounds as well as deaf people or people with learning or language difficulties. Similarly, websites that follow a consistent pattern and are simple to use make it easier for the elderly to come to terms with an unfamiliar medium and make the most of the advantages of the Internet for their everyday lives.

The design of accessible websites involves the separation of content and presentation. This is achieved using so-called *Cascading Style Sheets*.[2] This is also of benefit to the website's providers as much less space is required on the server to store the web pages and less traffic generated to load them. It also means that a fu-

Controlling the computer using a headmouse that records head movement as well as other input devices.

ture relaunch – i.e., a revision and redesign – of the web service is less complex and therefore also less costly.

No progress without enforcement – policies and statutory basis

At a European level, the eEurope Action Plans from 2002 and 2005 required providing equal opportunities for people with disabilities. Although all member states were requested to implement the action plans, this process has progressed differently in the individual countries. For example, equality for disabled persons has been regulated in Great Britain since 1995 by the "Disability Discrimination Act," in Spain by the "Ley 51 de igualdad de oportunidades, no discriminación y accesibilidad" ratified in 2003, in France since 2005 by the "Loi pour l'égalité des droits et des chances, la participation et la citoyenneté des personnes handicapées," and in Austria by the "Behindertengleichstellungsgesetz" which came into force on 1 January 2006. Other European countries have issued only guidelines or agreements and have no statutory basis how to achieve these aims.

In Germany, the version of the "Bundesbehindertengleichstellungsgesetz" (BGG, Disability Equality Act) that came into force in 2002 was the first statutory basis for regulating the accessibility of information and communication technologies. This encompassed an inclusive understanding of accessibility that rejects the provision of special alternative or partial solutions for specific user groups.

According to § 4 of the BGG, "[...] information processing systems, auditory and visual information resources and communication facilities, and any other areas which are designed, [are accessible when they are] usable by disabled people in the usual way, without any particular difficulty and, fundamentally, without external assistance from other people."

§ 11 of the BGG regulates "Accessible Information Technology" and stipulates that all websites, publicly accessible intranet and graphical programme interfaces provided by public institutions must be designed so that they can be used by disabled people without any restrictions. While the BGG applies to all national public authorities, the federal structure of Germany means that all German states have their own corresponding statutory regulations for their own public authorities. The regulations set out in the BGG are recommended for the private sector, but are not mandatory. Instead, the law provides an instrument known as a "target agreement." This allows certain organisations and interest groups that are certified by the responsible ministry to request private sector providers to enter into "target agreement negotiations." Private sector providers are then obliged to take part in the negotiations and failure to enter into or observe an agreement can be juridically prosecuted. According to German law, such legal action can only be taken by the aforementioned organisations, not by private persons.

In Austria, for example, the situation is different. The Austrian "Behindertengleichstellungsgesetz" is likewise applicable for all public authorities but also for private websites where these are "concerned with accessing and providing goods and services which are available to

....

2   *The Cascading Style Sheets* (CSS) formating language was developed in the early 1990s to describe how content on the web is presented. c.f. http://www.w3.org/Style/CSS

3   c.f. http://www.egalite-handicap.ch/deutsch/gleichstellungs-recht

4   Bühler, Christian (ed.), *Barrierefreies Webdesign. Praxishandbuch für Webgestaltung und grafische Programmoberflächen*, dpunkt-Verlag, Heidelberg 2005, p. 6.

the public" and where "direct state regulatory competence is given" (§2). This means that accessibility can be enforced wherever the Austrian consumer protection legislation ("Konsumentenschutzgesetz") applies. In effect, this permits a level of enforcement similar to the *Americans with Disabilities Act* (ADA) in the USA which allows private persons to take legal action and can – as with similar action in other fields – involve extraordinarily high compensation claims. Equal opportunities for people with disabilities in sections of public administration in the USA is regulated by "Section 508 of the Workforce Rehabilitation Act" as amended in 1998. This law requires US federal departments and agencies to ensure that their websites are accessible and to only procure, develop and employ information and communication technology that is also accessible and usable by people with disabilities.

In Germany, the term "Barrierefreies Webdesign" denotes the design of accessible websites and services as elaborated in the "Barrierefreie Informationstechnik-Verordnung" (BIT V, Barrier-free Information Technology Regulation), which is a supplementary regulation that came into effect in 2002 to augment § 11 of the BGG and governs technical implementation. Internationally one speaks of *Web Content Acces-* *sibility*. Both terms describe the same basic principle of ensuring "the technical accessibility of software along with observance of the fundamental principles of software ergonomics."[4]

On an international level, the requirements of accessible web design are defined in the *Web Content Accessibility Guidelines* (WCAG) developed by the *Web Accessibility Initiative* (WAI)[5] . The German BIT V is based on the first edition WCAG 1.0 of these guidelines. A completely revised version 2.0 of the WCAG has since been issued in December 2008.[6] A corresponding revision of the German BIT V is being undertaken by the Federal Ministry for Labour and Social Affairs (BMAS) and is planned for release some time in 2009.

Accessibility as a matter of principle – the basics of accessible web design

For a better understanding of what accessible information and communication technologies means, it is useful to examine the principles of accessibility detailed in the *Web Content Accessibility Guidelines* that are carefully formulated independent from any special technology in use.[7] These four principles clearly illustrate the diversity of requirements that are people with different impairments have.

Perceptibility: This principle aims to ensure that all website content and functionality on a website is presented in such a way that it can be perceived by all users. The only exception is content that cannot be expressed or circumscribed in words.

Operability: To ensure that websites can be used, all interface components must be operable by any user, wherever possible without the need for special input devices. It is also important that all functionalities can be accessed from a keyboard – i.e. without a mouse – and is not subject to any time restrictions. Moving interface components should be avoided in general.

Understandability: The ability to easily and quickly navigate and move around within a website and the user interface is key to the successful use of any web-based content. Information presented through a website and the user interface should be easy to understand and intuitive to use. Site designers must take into account that people learn in different ways and have different backgrounds and levels of experience in using web-based services.

Robustness: This principle is intended to ensure that the web technologies employed are robust enough to allow a website to be accessed with current and future access technologies (browsers, assistive technologies). Interoperabil-ity and compatibility with common products should also be ensured.

The table opposite illustrates the kinds of barriers disabled people face with regard to the principles of perceptibility, operability and understandability. The crosses denote pre-existing barriers and minus signs denote barriers that cannot be overcome, while a plus sign indicates which kinds of representation are advantageous for respective user groups. Where both minus and plus symbols appear in the same row, users with different impairments have conflicting demands for that respective means of presentation, which need to be resolved.

In the evaluation prodedure of the BIENE Award for best-practice examples of accessible websites in German language, in addition to the WAI principles also criteria including *orientation, relevance of the content*, an *inclusive approach* and *design* are of relevance. This ensures that websites fulfil not only accessibility criteria but also apply to general quality requirements as well as ethic and aesthetic criteria.

The BIENE Award for accessible website design

Since 2003, the Stiftung Digitale Chancen[8] (Digital Opportunities Foundation) and Aktion Mensch[9] (German Association for the Care of

....

5   http://www.w3.org/WAI.new

6   http://www.w3.org/2008/12/wcag20-pressrelease.html (last accessed: 23/02/2009).

7   The WCAG 2.0 guidelines use the terms: *perceivable, operable, understandable*, http://www.w3.org/TR/2008/REC-WCAG20-20081211

8   www.digitale-chancen.de

9   www.aktion-mensch.de

	Blind	Partially sighted / colour blind	Deaf / hard of hearing	Learning or reading difficulties	Restricted motor functions
Graphical content	–		+	+	
Inability to scale content		x		x	
Colour contrast		x			
Mouse-dependent navigation	x	x			x
"Cramped" navigation					x
Audio/video content	–		x	+	
Time limits	x		x	x	x
Complex structure	x	x	x	x	
Complex language			x	x	

Barriers to accessing web content.

the Disabled) have organised a regular competition for the best accessible German-language websites. The acronym BIENE stands for "Barrierefreies Internet eröffnet neue Einsichten" (a barrier-free Internet reveals new insights; *Biene* also means "bee" in German) and promotes communication, joint action and productive cooperation.

Entries to the competition can be made in a number of different categories which correspond to the type of web service. The degree of complexity of each website is taken into account in the evaluation procedure as experience has shown that this plays a substantial role in the implementation of accessibility requirements. The competition differentiates between *information and communication websites, research and service websites, shopping and transaction websites* and *community and interactive websites*.

In 2005, a special junior award was introduced for student and trainee web developers.

All websites submitted to the competition are subjected to a multi-stage evaluation procedure. In the first stage, all websites that do not fulfil the basic requirements of accessibility are eliminated. The remaining entries then undergo a fine-test undertaken twice by two different assessors. The assessors apply the criteria and evaluation steps detailed in the BIENE-Catalogue to the relevant content and functionality of each website. Those websites that score highly with both assessors are then tested in practice situations by people with different disabilities. The users first test how easy it is to follow through a sequence of actions step by step and are then asked to undertake a general global task.

The evaluation procedure is monitored by a professional board comprising disabled users

The BIENE Award trophies.

and experts who then draw up a shortlist of the very best candidates for the final jury. Finally, the jury awards a gold, silver and bronze BIENE to the top three websites in each category, taking into account not only accessibility but also aspects of general quality and design. The jury also decides on the awarding of special prizes for sites that address the needs of particular user groups. Sponsorship prizes can also be awarded to operators of non-commercial websites, such as associations or self-help groups, providing services or content of public interest. Most of the winners of a BIENE Award go further than merely fulfilling statutory and technical minimum requirements for accessibility and the competition's assessment criteria; they build on these as a basis for developing innovative and creative solutions. Websites that are awarded a BIENE can be regarded as best-practice examples. A list of all prize winners is available online on www.biene-wettbewerb.de.

Web 2.0 – participative Internet

The term Web 2.0 has become synonymous with the emergence of new kinds of Internet services that aim to involve the end user more actively. The most well-known of these are *weblogs*, or *blogs* for short: online journals that can be published with the help of Internet-based programmes and do not require any prior web knowledge. Visitors are able to comment on journal entries and see their comments published in real time. Initially predominantly private diaries, blogs are now also used as an instrument for business communication or political expression. In the 2008 US presidential election, blogs by and about the political candidates played a key role in the campaign. The ability for end users to publish content themselves is a central characteristic of web 2.0 applications, as epitomised by so-called *wikis*. The online-encyclopaedia *Wikipedia*, whose entries are written by the Internet community, is perhaps the most well-known example of a wiki. Online office applications, mapping applications and online surveys and voting systems that reflect the opinions of visitors in real time as well as so-called *mash-ups*, in which end users are able to assemble information from different web servers according to their own needs, are further examples of web 2.0 services. Many of the above mentioned elements are integrated into interactive community platforms. While services such as Flickr or YouTube primarily facilitate the quick and easy publication of images or video for cost-free exchange with others, portals such as Facebook or StudiVZ allow people to publish a profile of themselves and make contact with other users.

A key characteristic of web 2.0 applications is the provision of functionality for creating and publishing content that could previously only be undertaken by website providers, using content-management systems for example. Now end users are able to create and publish content inside other websites – the user can switch from being a recipient to a producer. This places new demands on the media literacy of the users as well as on the design of web services and the accessibility of the functionality they offer. When one considers the aforementioned principles published by the WAI – perceptibility, operability, understandability and robustness – it becomes clear that the accessible design of services such as social-community platforms presents developers with entirely new challenges.

Websites that offer content that was previously created by predominantly professional content producers can – at least to a degree – through legislation be obliged to fulfil accessibility standards. The same does not apply to so-called *user-generated content* as well as web applications with a stronger focus on interaction or communication. In view of the rapid development of the Internet and the increasing availability of web 2.0 services, BIENE undertook a

study in 2007 to examine the user behaviour of people with disabilities when using such services, with the intention of further development of the catalogue of criteria for accessible web design from the findings. The study consisted of three steps. In an initial exploratory stage, interviews were conducted with experts to ascertain a basic understanding of general patterns of Internet usage and the respective communication cultures of the different disabled user groups. In a second stage, group interviews were conducted with actual users of different disabled user groups to understand their motivations when using the Internet, their most favourite websites and online habits. Based on the findings of these two qualitative steps, a questionnaire was developed for implementation as an accessible online survey. 10 experts took part in the expert interviews, 57 disabled users in the group interviews, and a total of 671 disabled users answered the online questionnaire.

Parallel to the evaluation of the qualitative and quantitative surveys, BIENE also examined the accessibility of typical web 2.0 services and potential barriers to their use. The findings were then used to revise the BIENE catalogue of evaluation criteria for accessible web design and to add new evaluation steps. The results of the study will be published in 2009.

Seeing with the ears, hearing with the eyes

People who hear with their eyes and see with their ears have very special skills but are nevertheless regarded by society as disabled. The provision of equal opportunities for the disabled is an aim for society as a whole and is anchored in the German BGG. Since 2002, when the accessibility of information and communication technologies was first laid down in legislation, the accessibility of web content has improved significantly and with it the ability of disabled people to participate in the information society. Nevertheless, large sections of the Internet remain inaccessible for the greater majority of people with disabilities. Further initiatives are still necessary to raise awareness and provide information on accessible web design. The message of the BIENE – that accessible web design benefits all web users – aims to further this course.

As web 2.0 services become increasingly widespread, a new situation begins to emerge that offers chances as well as risks for people with disabilities. The BIENE study on web 2.0 services testifies to the high level of interest in such services among disabled people. To fully realise Internet accessibility, the end users themselves are called upon to ensure that their own *user-generated content* is also accessible. The digital inclusion of people with disabilities is something that we all can contribute to.

Further reading

BSI, Bundesamt für Sicherheit in der Informationstechnologie, *e-Government-Handbuch*; www.bsi.de/fachthem/egov/3.htm

Christian Bühler (ed.), *Barrierefreies Webdesign, Praxishandbuch für Webgestaltung und grafische Programmoberflächen*, dpunkt-Verlag, Heidelberg 2005.

Joe Clark, *Building Accessible Websites,* New Riders Publishing, Indianapolis 2003.

Jutta Croll, Ulrike Peter, "Benutzergerechte und zugängliche Gestaltung von Internetanwendungen für Senioren", in: Clemens Schwender (ed.), *Technikdokumentation für Senioren*, Schmidt-Römhild, Lübeck 2005 (tekom Hochschulschriften, vol. 12).

Wolfgang Dzida, "Qualitätssicherung durch software-ergonomische Normen", in: Edmund Eberleh, Horst Oberquelle, Reinhard Oppermann (ed.), *Einführung in die Software-Ergonomie*, deGryuter, Berlin 1994, pp. 373–406.

Gesetz zur Gleichstellung behinderter Menschen. Date of issue April 27, 2002, BGBI I 2002, 1468; field of reference: FNA 860-9-2, GESTA G086, changed by Art. 210 V of November 25, 2003 I 2304; www.bundesrecht.juris.de/bundesrecht/bgg

ISO/TS 16071: Ergonomics of human-system interaction – Guidance on accessibility for human-computer interfaces.

National Telecommunications and Information Administration (NTIA), *Falling through the Net*, 1995; 1998; 1999; 2000: www.ntia.doc.gov

Jakob Nielsen, *Designing Web Usability: The Practice of Simplicity*, New Riders Publishing, Indianapolis 2000.

Reinhard Oppermann, Harald Reiterer, "Software-ergonomische Evaluation," in: Edmund Eberleh, Horst Oberquelle, Reinhard Oppermann (ed.), *Einführung in die Software-Ergonomie*, deGryuter, Berlin 1994, pp. 335–371.

Angie Radtke, Michael Charlier, *Barrierefreies Webdesign*, Addison-Wesley Verlag, Munich 2006.

Peter Rainger, "Dyslexic Perspective on E-Content Accessibility", available online under: www.techdis.ac.uk/seven/papers/dyslexia.html

Christa Schlenker-Schulte (ed.): *Barrierefreie Information und Kommunikation. Hören – Sehen – Verstehen in Arbeit und Alltag*, Neckar Verlag, Villingen-Schwenningen 2004 (Wissenschaftliche Beiträge aus Forschung, Lehre und Praxis zur Rehabilitation von Menschen mit Behinderungen).

Beate Schulte, Ulrike Peter, Jutta Croll, Iris Cornelssen, "Methodologies to identify best practice in barrier-free web design", in: *European Journal of E-Practice*, May 2008.

Constantine Stephanidis, *User Interfaces for All: Concepts, Methods, and Tools*, Lawrence Erlbaum Associates, Mahwah, NJ 2001.

Jim Thatcher et. al., *Accessible Web Sites*, glasshaus, Birmingham 2002.

Competition –
The Schindler Award and the culture of education
Thomas Sieverts

Since 2004, Schindler, the international manufacturer of elevators and escalators based in Lucerne, Switzerland, has organised a competition for schools of architecture in Europe entitled *Access for All*. Its aim: to foster greater sensibility towards the needs of disabled people in the city and in buildings among architectural schools in Europe. Simultaneously, it helps improve practical knowledge and skills in planning and implementing building measures that make a lasting contribution to a better quality of life for everyone, not just for people with disabilities. From its inception, the goal of the competition has been to enable people with different abilities to enjoy the same conditions of access, rather than to separate them by using dedicated technical solutions.

Right from the beginning, response to the announcement of the competition was considerable: in 2004, 72 architectural schools from throughout Europe with a total of 497 students took part, and by 2008, the third iteration of the competition, this had risen to 95 architectural schools and a total of 957 students – from Yekaterinburg in the Ural mountains to Madrid in Spain, from Lund in Sweden to Naples in Italy. The competition projects to date have considered a wider urban environment with special focus on the design of a large building. The first project was a planning task in Brussels fol-

lowed in the second competition by a project in Paris. The last project was located in Vienna. The winners are invited by Schindler to attend a gala ceremony in Lucerne. The public award ceremony therefore becomes an opportunity for talented, enterprising and adventurous architectural students and their teachers to meet and exchange experiences. Alongside architects and specialists for planning and building for the needs of the disabled, the jury also consists of experts in the field who are themselves disabled.

The results to date are somewhat ambivalent. The architectural quality of the designs in the upper third, and of the winners in particular, have for the most part been of a high-quality. Certain characteristic differences are apparent, for example with regard to the different architectural cultures in the respective countries and the individual learning cultures of the schools. With regard to the specific issue of *Access for All*, one can detect an increase in conceptual approaches to the issue from competition to competition but overall it is evident that students in general have only a limited awareness of the issue. A primary reason for this is that designing and planning for the needs of the disabled, not to mention *Access for All*, is rarely an integral part of architectural teaching and not communicated or practised systematically in design

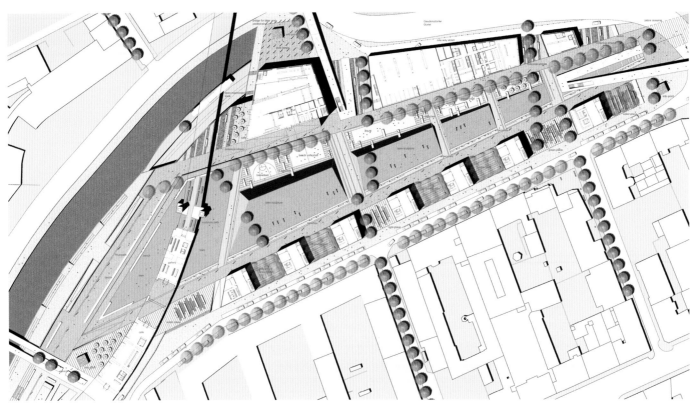

Layout showing the "service wedge," "green wedge," and the southern "housing wedge."

project work. Almost none of the courses include exercises in which students simulate the experience of being disabled themselves, for example by spending 24 hours in a wheelchair with restricted vision, although this has been demonstrated to be the most effective way of helping designers properly understand and internalise the problems disabled people face. For this reason, participating architectural schools will in future be required to offer a more committed teaching programme in this field.

To qualify for the University Award, institutions must fulfil the following conditions:

- Schools should participate with at least twelve students.
- Students must receive ongoing tutoring and support during the competition.
- Schools must offer at least two specific lectures and one seminar or workshop on the topic of accessibility.
- Schools must undertake an internal pre-selection of the most qualified students.

Architectural schools that fulfil these conditions qualify for the University Award totalling 25,000 Euro. The first *Schindler Award for Archi-*

....

Schindler Award 2008: Design for the redevelopment of a derelict area in centre of Vienna, Austria.
First Prize: University of Applied Sciences, Coblence
Students: Nils Krieger, Thorsten Stelter
Professor/lecturer: Eva von Mackensen, Sabine Hopp

Material & design of different speed zones and "lawn sculptures."

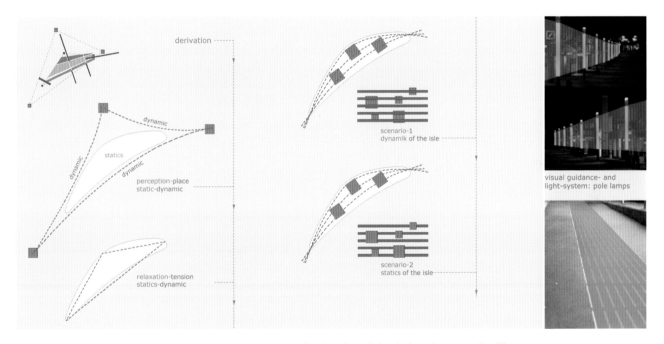

Conceptual plan derived from a triangular field of "tension and relaxation." Tactile and visual orientation system for different types of impairment.

North-east view of the riverside park with the community centre. View from the east showing the openness of the project. The riverside park with the vibrant community center.

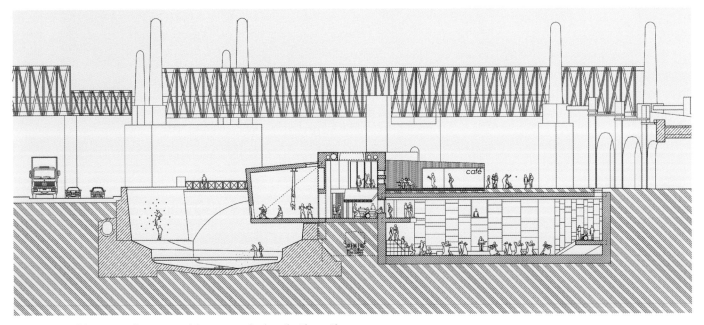

Cross-section of the community centre and the promenade along the Vienna River.

....

Schindler Award 2008: Design for the redevelopment of a derelict area in centre of Vienna Austria.
Second Prize: Czech Technical University, Prague – Faculty of Architecture
Students: Jakub Krcmar, Martina Sotkovska
Professor: Ivan Plicka

tecture was won in 2006 by the Bauhaus-Universität Weimar. In 2008, the prize was awarded to Koblenz University of Applied Sciences.

Overall, however, experience to date has shown that lasting improvements to architectural education in this area, both in teaching and in research, are not realistically to be expected in the short term: further patience is obviously required! This need not be a cause for despair if we consider the experiences of two other reform movements: the organic food movement and green building movement. Both first emerged some 25 years ago as the product of small groups of near-sectarian character. Driven by a strong belief in the greater, global relevance of their mission, they began with practical experiments and by adopting a way of life in accordance with their beliefs, well aware of the fact that much of society would at first be derisive of their endeavours.

Some time later, a dramatic turning point in public opinion came about which enabled the small, sectarian groups to be seen in a new light: what were once the opinions of a fringe group became more and more a key aspect of larger socio-political debate. As their beliefs became mainstream concerns they were taken up in the manifestos of the leading political parties. In the case of the green building movement, it was a growing awareness of environmental pollu-

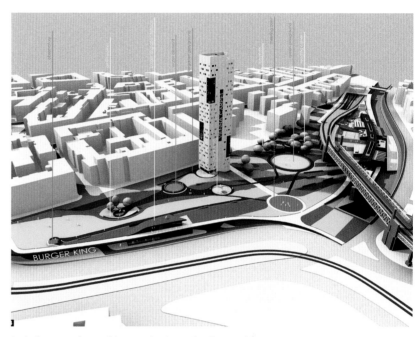

A sloping green "carpet" is spread out over the site, creating a large public space.

tion on the one hand and the climate and energy crisis on the other that propelled the principles of ecological building into the mainstream of political debate and ultimately into legislation. In the case of the organic food movement, wider general environmental consciousness and the impact of environmental scares on public awareness were responsible for bringing or-

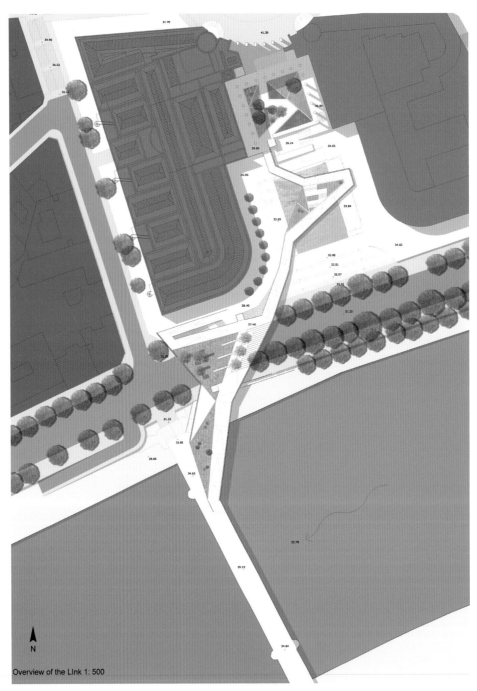

N

Overview of the Link 1: 500

The zigzag band adheres to permissible gradient guidelines.

....

Schindler Award 2006: Design for a barrier-free museum walk in Paris, France.
First Prize: Technical University of Vienna, Austria
Students: Marco di Nallo, Marta Neic, Manfred Sponseiler
Professor: Dörte Kuhlmann

View from the upper courtyard.

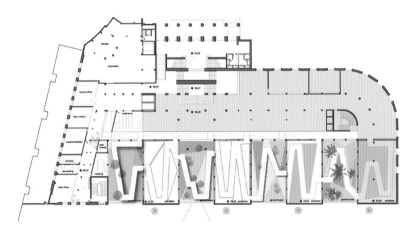

The zigzag band continues in the interior of the Palais de Tokyo.

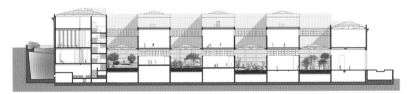

The path of discovery leads alternately through the courtyards and interior spaces.

The pathway begins at the pavilion, crosses the Seine, embraces the Palais de Tokyo, and ends in the driveway.

The pavilion is a resting place on the museum promenade, as well as a belvedere and boat station.

....

Schindler Award 2006: Design for a barrier-free museum walk in Paris, France.
Second Prize: Technical University of Delft, The Netherlands
Students: Adam Beard, Marie Henrike Haase
Professor: Kurt van Belle

ganically farmed produce back into public demand, lending weight in the process to a new slow food movement. *Access for All* must similarly transcend the narrower technical and geometric aspects of accessibility and become a central concern of a movement committed to humanist urban design and architecture: a movement that adds a physical and sensory component to the conventional notion of functionalism and is committed to creating a dignified living environment for everyone including those with restricted physical, sensory, mental, and often also economic means.

A movement of this kind must also incorporate principles of Universal Design, which aim primarily to address the needs and limitations of old people, and where possible to exceed these. At the same time, it should strive to create spaces in the public realm that especially allow children and young people to develop, experiment and experience – spaces that previously existed as open land and niches in the city but which have successively disappeared as a result of the total commercialisation of the city.

In today's architectural schools, the current movement promoting *Access for All* is still very small and barely visible. Among the few exceptions are daring attempts to postulate an architecture that is able to respond to the needs of its residents, sometimes in the form of hybrid com-

The former dreary back of the Palais changes into an exciting showcase for the senses.

binations of architecture and electronic media. With time, persistence in this field will pay off: as life expectancy increases while the population simultaneously declines, the elderly and very elderly, with their health and mobility problems, will grow to become one of the largest sections of society, and will increasingly be able to assert their particular interests politically. As with the ecology movement described earlier,

Access for All will become a mainstream concern, and in turn politically and economically viable once it acquires general political significance.

Paradoxically, increasing political pressure by the elderly generation to reform the city and public space in particular will also benefit children and young people. Somewhat simplified: what is good for old people can also be made good for young people and with it give rise to intergenerational environments throughout the city.

The Schindler Award *Access for All* will need to demonstrate staying power, vitality and persistence in its campaigning in order to convince and motivate architectural schools in Europe to propagate the design of a humanist environment of the kind this award stands for.

Appendix –
The Authors

Gernot Böhme, born in 1937 in Dessau, studied mathematics, physics and philosophy, gaining his doctorate in Hamburg in 1965 and post-doctorate (Habilitation) in Munich in 1972. From 1970-1977 he worked as a researcher at the Max Planck Institute in Starnberg investigating the living conditions of the scientific and technical world. In 1977 Böhme became professor of philosophy at the TU Darmstadt, a position he held until 2002. He has been a guest professor in Australia, England, Japan, Austria, the Netherlands, Sweden and the USA. From 1997 to 2001, he was spokesman for the postgraduate programme "Technology and Society" in Darmstadt. In 2003 he was awarded the Prize of Philosophy of the Denkbar Foundation in Frankfurt. Since 2005, he has been director of the Institute for Philosophical Practice (IPPh) in Darmstadt.

Wolfgang Christ (Prof. Dipl.-Ing.) was born in 1951 in Engers on the Rhine. After studying architecture at the TH Darmstadt, he worked from 1983 to 1988 as an academic assistant as part of the "City Task Group" with Professor Thomas Sieverts. From 1989 to 1993 he was a lecturer at the TH Darmstadt, among other things for Urban Design and New Media. In 1994, Wolfgang Christ was appointed Professor for Urban Planning and Urban Design at the Faculty of Architecture at the Bauhaus-Universität Weimar. As one of the co-founders of the "European Urban Studies" postgraduate study programme, Wolfgang Christ was also Director of the Institute for European Urban Studies (IfEU) from 2006 to 2008. He also runs his own office for architecture and urbanism, "Mediastadt – Urban Strategies," founded in 1989. He lectures at the International Real Estate Business School (IREBS) in

Regensburg, and is a member of the Architecture Committee of the Cultural Circle of German Business and Industry within the Federation of German Industry. Wolfgang Christ is co-editor of the ZIÖ, *Journal of Real Estate Economics*, and the "Shopping-Center-Stadt" series of publications. He has published extensively and lectures widely on new developments in urbanism. During his academic career he has received numerous awards including the EDRA/Places Award (USA, 2001) and the German Urban Design Prize Special Award (Deutsche Städtebaupreis, Sonderpreis, 2006). In 2008 he founded the Urban INDEX Institute which focuses on the analysis and certification of the qualities of urban environments.

Jutta Croll, born in 1956, works as a scientist and researcher on a variety of projects concerning the use of media and promotion of media competencies. From 1985 to 1990, she studied German literature, politics and media science at the University of Göttingen, Germany, and has worked as a freelance consultant to the German UNESCO Commission and the Brockhaus Encyclopedia. In April 2003 she became managing director of the Stiftung Digitale Chancen (Digital Opportunities Foundation), a non-profit organisation that promotes equal access to the internet and media competencies.

Susanne Edinger (Prof. Dr.-Ing.) was born in 1956 in Bad Kreuznach and studied town and regional planning at the University of Kaiserslautern, working with and completing her doctorate under Professor Albert Speer. She has seven years experience as an architect, working in all phases, and is also trained as a systemic coach. Since 1994, she has been Professor for Urban Design, Development Planning and Project Development at the Faculty of Architecture and Engineering at the SRH University of Applied Sciences in Heidelberg.

Jonas Hughes, born in 1967 in Johannesburg, South Africa, is a journalist, broadcaster and communications specialist. He has worked for various newspapers, broadcasters and online publishers in South Africa, Canada, Britain and Switzerland. For five years he was magazine editor and news journalist at the BBC World Service in London before moving to Bern, Switzerland, where he spent seven years with swissinfo, the overseas arm of the Swiss Broadcasting Corporation, most recently as head of the English-language service. Since January 2007 he has been Group Chief Editor at the Schindler Group in Ebikon, Switzerland.

Willi Loose, born in 1952 in Frankfurt a.M., became managing director of the German National Car Sharing Association (Bundesverbandes CarSharing e.V.), the umbrella organisation for all German car sharing operators, in 2006. He trained as a secondary school teacher, specialising in political studies and biology. For many years he was a member of the research staff at the Transport and Infrastructure Division of the Institute for Applied Ecology in Freiburg.

Tobias Reinhard (Dipl.-Arch. ETH/SIA/SWB), born in 1952 in Bern, Switzerland, trained as an architect at the ETH Swiss Federal Institute of Technology in Zurich. From 1982 to 2002 he was a partner in the architectural office Reinhard + Partner AG Bern, since 2002, partner and project developer with Nüesch Development AG. In

2003, he took over the architectural management of the Schindler Award. He is also a board member of the Swiss Center for Accessible Building for the Disabled.

Anna Rose (Dipl.-Ing.) was born in 1974 in Darmstadt and studied architecture at the RWTH Aachen and the Bartlett School, University College London. She has professional experience in various architectural practices in Germany, the UK, and the US. In 2007, Anna became a director of consultancy with the urban planning consultancy Space Syntax Limited. She has developed a specialism in urban design, and public realm design. She is the author of numerous publications and lectures to architectural audiences both in the UK and internationally, and has taught specialised seminars at various universities. She is involved in worldwide project collaborations of all scales.

Thomas Sieverts (Prof. emeritus) was born in 1934 in Hamburg and studied architecture and urban design in Stuttgart, Liverpool, and Berlin, graduating in 1962. Together with Egbert Kossak and Herbert Zimmermann he founded the "Freie Planungsgruppe Berlin" in 1967. From 1967 to 1999, he has worked as a professor of urban design at universities in Berlin, Nottingham, and Darmstadt, also working concurrently as an architect from his office in Bonn from 1967 to 2005. He is the author of numerous publications.

Jeannot Simmen, born in 1946 in Switzerland, is an author, exhibition curator and book editor. He studied art history, philosophy and theology in Zurich and Berlin before training at the State Museums Prussian Cultural Heritage Foundation in Berlin. He undertook his postdoctoral thesis on *Vertigo – Das Entstehen moderner Kunst aus dem irritierten Gleichgewicht* at the University of Wuppertal. He has been guest and stand-in professor for art history and design theory in Berlin, Kassel, Wuppertal and Essen, and is founder and chairman of the "Club Bel Etage Berlin." He has curated numerous exhibitions, projects and publications focussing on culture, new media and the visual arts.

Cord Soehlke (Dipl.-Ing), born in 1969 in Bielefeld, studied architecture in Kassel and has worked as a press and television journalist. In 1997 he joined the Südstadt development agency in Tübingen, becoming project manager for urban redevelopment measures in 2001 and head of the Tübingen Urban Development Department. In 2003, he was also appointed managing director of the Tübingen Economic Development Agency (WIT, Wirtschaftsfördergesellschaft Tübingen), focussing on the urban redevelopment of brownfield sites. He has published numerous articles, sits in competition juries, lectures and provides consultancy for local authorities.

Tim Stonor, born in 1968 in Newcastle upon Tyne, studied architecture and town planning at the Bartlett School, University College London, and at Oxford Brookes University. In 1996 he set up the consulting firm Space Syntax Limited. As managing director Tim oversees the practice's consulting activities and is responsible for the strategic direction of the business in the UK and overseas. Tim is a member of the Design Review Panel of the UK Commission for Architecture and the Built Environment (CABE) and a director of the UK Academy of Urbanism. He speaks frequently at industry conferences throughout the world and is a regular contributor to television and radio programmes on architecture and design.

John Thompson is an architect and town planner and founder of John Thompson & Partners, London, as well as president of the British Academy of Urbanism. He has extensive experience of urban regeneration and residential development. Since the 1980s, he has pioneered the development of community planning as a tool for professional town planning with a view to achieving better and more lasting planning objectives in the private and public sectors. He has undertaken masterplanning and collaborative urban design projects in the UK, Ireland, Iceland, Russia, Germany, France, Sweden, the United Arab Emirates and China.

Andreas von Zadow, born in 1958 in Bad Hersfeld, Germany, studied communication sciences at the TU Berlin, graduating in 1984. He is a moderator and consultant for participative planning processes. He worked for five years at the City of Berlin's Department for Urban Development, and was vice president of the European Academy of the Urban Environment (EA.UE) for two years. In 1996 his "Perspektivenwerkstatt" method for community planning was introduced throughout the German-speaking nations. In 2000 he became managing director of VON ZADOW GmbH – Interactive Urban Development and has since undertaken some of the largest community planning projects in Germany, including projects in Munich, Essen, Leverkusen, Arnsberg, Ludwigsfelde, Berlin and Lübeck. He organises and chairs workshops, large-scale community planning projects, EU projects and world congresses.

Appendix –
Illustration credits

Adam Beard, Marie Henrike Haase 178, 179
Bundesverband CarSharing eV (bcs) 136
cambio Mobilitätsservice GmbH & Co.KG 135
Car Sharing Italia S.r.l. 141
Chichester District Council 51 right
Wolfgang Christ 98 left, 99–101, 103, 108, 110
CP/compartner, Ralph Lueger 109 left
Daimler AG 140 right
Uwe Drepper 25
Dublin City Council 45, 46 right
Susanne Edinger 114, 115 right, 118, 119 right
Susanne Edinger, Helmut Lerch 115 left
Galerie nationale du Jeu de Paume 19
Wolfram Gothe 31–42
Manfred Grohe 76
Valentin Hadelich 137
Werner J. Hannapel 107
HEINZ-Magazin Verlags GmbH 109 right
Invers GmbH 140 left
ITV plc 26
Wolfram Janzer 119 left
John Thompson & Partners (JTP) 47, 50, 51 left,
    51 middle, 52, 53, 56 bottom, 57, 58 left, 60
John Thompson & Partners (JTP), Metropolitan
    Workshop 46 left
Jakub Krcmar, Martina Sotkovska 174, 175
Nils Krieger, Thorsten Stelter 172, 173
Willi Loose 113, 142
Stadt Lübeck 58 rechts, 59 right
Stadt Lübeck, Petersen Pörksen Partner 59 left
Gudrun de Maddalena 68
Mobility Center GmbH, teilAuto Erfurt 139
Marco di Nallo, Marta Neic, Manfred Sponseiler
    176, 177
Marie-Lan Nguyen 151, 154

Nicholls & Clarke 116
Otis Elevator Company 20 right
OTIS GmbH & Co. OHG 20 left
Philadelphia Museum of Art, Walter and Louise
    Arensberg Collection 27
Rehavista GmbH, www.rehavista.de 161
Hartmut Reiche, Aktion Mensch 160, 166
Tobias Reinhard 128, 132, 133 left
Schindler Aufzüge AG 31–35, 38–43
Schweizerischer Gewerkschaftsbund SGB,
    133 right
Siemens-Archiv 21
Archiv Simmen/Drepper 18, 22, 23, 24
Cord Soehlke 64, 71–73
Space Syntax Limited 81–93
SPIEGEL-Verlag Rudolf Augstein GmbH & Co.
    KG 109 middle
Sussman/Prejza & Co. 95, 96
Tandrige District Council 56 top
Universitätsstadt Tübingen 63, 65–67, 69, 70,
    74, 75
Urbis Manchester 102
VG Bild-Kunst, Bonn 2009 17
VON ZADOW GmbH 49, 54–55
Erik Weber 98 right
Messer Woland 29

Every effort has been made to trace the copy-rightholders, architects, and designers and we apologise in advance for any unintentional omission and would be pleased to insert the appropriate acknowledgement in any subsequent edition.